SILHOUETTE IN THE EBBING TIDE

by

Ron Gerlach

Phelsuma Press
2016

Also by Ron Gerlach:
  Footprints in Shifting Sand
  The Lost Giants: a tale of tortoises in the Seychelles
  Raising Happy Giant Tortoises

Written & illustrated by the author:
  An Island Lost in Time
  The Tortoise who Thought he was a Dodo (a book for children)

all available from http://wildlife-art.org

ISBN: 978-0-9932203-2-6

Phelsuma Press, Cambridge
© R. Gerlach 2016

SILHOUETTE IN THE EBBING TIDE

by

Ron Gerlach

"Conservation? It will break your heart."
- Betty Beckett 1984

CHAPTER ONE

The fierce north-west wind that had lashed the sea, tearing the white crests from the mountainous waves, suddenly abated as though Aeolus, father of the winds, had reined in his unruly son. The turbulent sea, so eager to respond to the first gusts of wind, would take days to subside, leaving the two storm-battered East India Company vessels to make slow passage across the Indian Ocean.

Their navigation by dead reckoning had gone awry during the heavy weather which had pushed them onto an unfamiliar course. In the early morning light, a strange uncharted island appeared, silhouetted against the rising sun. If this was one of the mysterious "Sete Irmaos" islands the Portuguese cartographers had included on their charts, then the ships were much further east than their navigator had intended.

The possibility of finding fresh water, fruit and game, inevitably drew the ships toward the island. As they approached their anticipation of making a landing began to fade; the island was a tall, steep forest-covered mountain reaching from its troubled rocky coast to a cloud-shrouded summit. This western headland was dominated by sheer rock faces plunging into deep water and further along the coast where the forest swept down to the edge of the sea, a formidable barrier of waves crashing over a coral reef persuaded them that this was no place to make landfall. They changed course towards a smaller, lower island lying close by on their port side.

On the north side of this smaller island they found a relatively calm bay where they heaved to, but were hesitant to drop anchor. A wide sandy beach with no protective coral reef lay within easy reach for a brief expedition to find fresh water. On landing, they pushed through the beach-crest vegetation into a natural amphitheatre; a wide plateau surrounded on three sides by steep rocky hills holding a small coastal forest in their embrace. They had seen sea-turtle tracks impressed into the soft sand of the beach but inland the turtles were replaced by numerous very large tortoises. Brown, as well as pure white terns fluttered through the trees, keeping up an incessant chatter, while turtle-doves the size of large pigeons busied themselves on the ground. The only water lay in an open marshy area frequented by the tortoises whose passage in and out of the marsh made the water unpalatable.

Concern about the safety of their temporary anchorage prompted them to head further east to where they had seen the blue-grey shadow of a larger island, where they hoped to find a sheltered anchorage. On their approach, they could make out turtle tracks on the beaches and several large tortoises sheltering in the beach-crest vegetation. Here too, white terns could be seen flying through the forest canopy and much larger white tropic-birds with their long streaming tails cruised above the higher altitude forest. In this world of nature, untouched by man, there were even large bats circling over the forest on the thermal currents in broad daylight; golden fox-like animals on outstretched leathery black wings.

When the ships resumed their passage late in January 1609, they carried with them a load of giant tortoises to supplement their meagre shipboard diet. Their harvest also included much needed fresh water, turtles, doves and coconuts, but they found no edible fruit. They had not touched the trees in the forest even though they had judged them to be perfect timber for ship repairs. The islands returned to being a natural paradise once more, as though they had never been disturbed by man.

Nearly 400 years later, on a day towards the end of the doldrums, when the monsoon winds were stilled and the trade-winds not yet aroused, that same first seen island (Silhouette) lay reflected in the sea ahead of us. The mountains that reached up into the low clouds were still covered in dense forest and we saw no sign of roads, nor any buildings on that day in May of 1997. It seemed as though little had changed in all the years since the island was first seen by the sailors on those two East India Company ships. But much had changed.

As far as we know, these "Sete Irmaos" islands remained lost, forgotten and uninhabited by humans until 1742 when a formal expedition was despatched from Mauritius to investigate the possible possession and subsequent settlement of the islands. In 1770, a small garrison was established in what became known as the Seychelles archipelago, ultimately providing the stepping stone for the occupation of the islands by French settlers.

In the same way as we were setting off on our journey to a new life on Silhouette island, in a boat loaded with all our belongings, the early settlers came to the islands equipped to survive. They brought with them the knowledge and the tools to build their houses and the seeds for the crops that would sustain them. While fish were plentiful and there were ample tortoises and turtles to eat, the only edible fruit were coconuts. To improve their diet, the settlers brought with them their cattle, goats, pigs and poultry and for companionship, their dogs, cats and, accidentally, their rats. They cleared the land to plant their crops, felled the trees to build their houses and imported agricultural plants to sustain their lives and livelihoods.

Land concessions were given to the settlers on the principal islands of Mahé, Praslin and La Digue, where the coastal plateaux were relatively wide and suitable for agriculture. There was only very limited flat land on Silhouette because of the steep terrain, making life very difficult for the few families who settled there. Their survival may have depended upon extraction of the valuable hardwood timber in the natural forest an essential for both house and boat building.

The impact the settlers had on the environment was first reported to the authorities in Mauritius by the surveyor Jean-Baptiste de Malavois in 1787. He carried out a thorough survey of the natural resources on all the islands and was concerned about the over-exploitation of the forests, the tortoises and the turtles. He proposed to the authorities that they set up a sanctuary on Cerf Island for the rapidly decreasing numbers of Seychelles giant tortoises, which proposal the authorities chose to ignore. He emphasised the need to reduce felling the hardwood forest on Silhouette and was aghast to find the vegetation on North Island destroyed by fire and the island overrun with rats, which may have been a legacy not of recent settlers, but dating back to the first visitors in 1609.

Among the land owners on Silhouette Island was a man called Auguste Dauban whose father was a medical doctor with several business interests in Mauritius. They owned a small vessel that traded between Mauritius and Seychelles. Auguste and his Irish wife, Catherine, realised that Silhouette had great potential if it were under one single owner, and made it their business gradually to buy out the other land owners when they fell on hard times. Thus it was that by the mid-nineteenth century they became the sole owners of the island.

Under their stewardship, the high forest was left untouched but the coastal plateaux and lower forests were cleared and planted with agricultural crops; coconut plantations on the flat land, cinnamon and fast-growing timber trees on the foothills. These commercial crops were only a fraction of the plants and trees that were introduced onto the island. All the tropical fruit trees needed to sustain life were planted in this once fruitless environment as were coffee, cocoa, rice, maize, spices and perfume plants. The once pristine environment had been manipulated to support mankind.

Auguste and Catherine built a large formal plantation house, the Grande Case, which had a commanding view of the main pass through the coral reef and of any approaching vessels. From the beach to the entrance to the pass they constructed a narrow stone jetty and a slipway for their boats. In these idyllic settings they raised their children, cared for their workers, ran a small school and a primitive clinic.

At the end of their long and busy lives they were finally laid to rest in a small neo-classical mausoleum not far from the Grande Case. A baby daughter and Catherine's sister share this tranquil resting place with them. After Auguste and Catherine, the island was managed by their daughters; their two sons having returned to Mauritius and France.

The last Dauban to look after the family interests on Silhouette was Auguste's grandson, Henri. He was an extraordinary character who, while studying the production of essential oils in England, was selected to represent Great Britain as a javelin thrower in the 1924 Paris Olympics. He brought the benefits of his agricultural education to Silhouette to boost the income needed to support a population of one thousand workers. He increased the production of copra by extending the coconut plantation into the lower reaches of the forest. Cinnamon, the second most important crop, was gradually invading all the forest areas. The fertile seeds were spread by the forest-inhabiting birds, like bulbuls and the introduced Indian mynahs. The high altitude marsh at Mare aux Cochons, the only such habitat on Silhouette, was channelled, drained and planted with coffee. He also cleared several areas of forest on the mountainside to create alien commercial timber plantations. High above La Passe on a small plateau known as Jardin Marron, he planted a grove of Coco de Mer trees.

The unexpected decline in the market price for copra (and hence coconut oil), caused by post-war cheap sources of vegetable oil from the industrial farms in America, began to erode the viability of copra production on many tropical islands. Henri slowly slipped into debt, despite heroic efforts to support his workers. In 1971 with the promise of major tourism development in Seychelles, Henri and the Indian merchant who had financed him were rescued by a large consortium of French individuals who bought Silhouette and took on the responsibility of supporting the decreasing population on the island. A coup d'état in 1977 brought their plans to a grinding halt and six years later the island was compulsorily purchased from the French owners by the government, and the ownership given to a government parastatal company.

As compensation for the loss of their investment, the French group, under the guidance of Jean-Jacques Fernier, were allowed to retain the lease on the Daubans' plantation house, the Grande Case. This proved to be a meaningless gesture as the house was not in any state to accommodate its wealthy lessees who chose instead to spend their holidays in the newly built Silhouette Island Lodge.

Our first visit to Silhouette had been a day trip in 1987 when the new owner, Island Development Company, had been in charge for about three years. In much the same way as the legacy from the one-party political era had left the islands under the control of one powerful person, so it was with Silhouette and the outer islands. This owner had established a large industrial-scale poultry farm at the northern end of La Passe and we were impressed by the new social centre, shop, clinic and cold store. There were several new houses including some interesting timber-log buildings. We had lunch at the Lodge; a small hotel that boasted twelve individual thatched chalets where Lorenza, the Italian architect, was putting the finishing touches to part of the hotel. We were there ostensibly to look for snails for our son, Justin's, snail guide. In the afternoon we re-embarked on the small boat that took us through the narrow winding pass in the reef to the big-game fishing boat that would take us back to Mahé.

The Oxford University Silhouette Expedition of 1990 was organised and led by Justin. His team consisted of four fellow biology students from Oxford; Caroline, Claire, Richard and Graham and included two people from Seychelles; Mo, a doctor friend, and Pat, a naturalist who worked in the broadcasting company. They had chosen to carry out a biodiversity assessment in an unusual high altitude *Pisonia* forest that had been discovered in 1986 by a French botanist, Francis Friedmann. This expedition was the first thorough biodiversity investigation to be undertaken on Silhouette since Hugh Scott's study at the time of the Percy Sladen Trust Expeditions of 1905.

Our house on Mahé was their base camp, a safe haven of warm baths, comfortable beds and proper meals when they needed a break from their three month-long period of camping in the high forest. As a reward, Gill and I were persuaded to visit their campsite and field lab on the mountain ridge above Jardin Marron, where Henri Dauban had planted the Coco de Mer Palms. It was a beautiful, tranquil area with a stream meandering between the scattered boulders. The Coco de Mer palms had not been planted close together and were more dispersed than we had thought. Between them grew several breadfruit trees and a small plantation of strange red-skinned bananas, all reminders of the escaped slaves, the "marrons" who had once tried to survive here.

There was a stretch of incredibly steep hillside above Jardin Marron that we had to traverse before reaching the camp; six damp-looking tents with bedding out in the sun to air and dry, plus a tarpaulin stretched between the trees acting as kitchen, dining and work room. While we recovered from our climb, we listened to the occasional high pitched peeping call of the tiny sooglossid frogs and the clacking of the white-tailed tropic birds that seemed to be nesting in the tall trees below the cliffs of La Chaine Catherine, the name Auguste had given to the ridge leading to Mont Dauban.

After a picnic lunch, we were shown the pressed plants they had collected, the insects, burrowing skinks and frogs. We wandered out onto a huge sheet of granite; a "glacis" as it is known in Seychelles, to admire the exceptional view of the mountains and the forest tumbling all the way down to Grande Barbe on the other side of the island. There followed a long scramble down to the hotel, the Silhouette Island Lodge, to give it is proper name, in preparation for our return trip to Mahé. Justin introduced us to Mario and Ornella Lapolla, the Italian couple who had taken on the lease of the Lodge.

There was a big lazy swell running along the old stone jetty as we set off into the south-east tradewind-disturbed sea with its flocks of noddy terns and skimming shearwaters.

The Silhouette Expedition with its discovery of the importance of the island and especially those high altitude forests for the biodiversity of the Seychelles, made us wonder how we could persuade the authorities that this natural treasure-house needed protection. It was, however, most unlikely in that era of dictatorial one party politics that any notice would be taken of a proposal from a member of the public.

Gill and I returned to our craftwork at the studio on Beau Vallon beach and watched the sunsets over Silhouette from our house at Le Niol. Justin returned to his studies at Oxford. At the end of term when he came home we went on excursions into the forest on Mahé collecting the endemic snails and recording the insects, plants and birds. Justin and I spent many hours counting the migrating shorebirds; making good use of the smart new telescope he had bought for me. The shorebirds prompted us to investigate the quality of their feeding grounds as these slowly relocated to new parts of the shallows, following the major land reclamation project all along the east cost of Mahé.

CHAPTER TWO

The incoming spring tide was gradually covering what remained of the once extensive sandbars and mudflats where the shorebirds hunted for polychaete worms and tiny molluscs. The first small bands of curlew sandpipers flew in, settling in fussy groups along the edge of the shallow freshwater ponds. Their numbers slowly built up to well over 150 before the larger waders, whimbrels and grey plovers, arrived. The turnstones had flown in earlier, as apparently had two greenshanks and a bar-tailed godwit. A dapper little green-backed heron was perched on an abandoned scaffold tube and from this vantage point he stared intently into the calm water.

The landscape that attracted these flocks of migratory water-birds was not some beautiful coastal marsh surrounded by lush tropical vegetation, it was instead a reminder of how humans desecrate nature in the name of development. Miles and miles of totally flat coral sand reclamation covered all the reef flats from the airport to the edge of Victoria; sand and coral dredged up from the seabed, destroying the tiny creatures, the crabs and hundreds of thousands of sea-shells that inhabited that underwater world.

Gone forever was the vast inter-tidal zone where the migrant shorebirds fed; reduced to mere strips of mudflat and sandbars, more silt than sand, hardly suitable for the large flocks of curlew sandpipers we had recorded in the past and which, in later years, would by-pass the islands altogether.

The shallow depression which the birds had adopted had been created during the dredging operations as a siltation pond where the dredger had spewed out its final load of silt-filled sea-water. This same large hole in the reclamation, so close to the town, had attracted not only the birds but also the solid waste agency that wished to use it as a convenient landfill site.

We thought there was a case to make for the protection of this high-tide roost for the migratory birds that used it – there were untold hectares of reclamation where the landfill site could be located, but only one safe place for the birds. The government-run daily newspaper gave me the whole of page three to set out a case for protecting the area for the birds. It was a happy coincidence that our campaign, if it could be called a campaign, occurred shortly after a visit to the Indian Ocean islands by French President, François Mitterand. It was he who persuaded the various island governments to turn their backs on their long-established one party political systems in favour of true democracy.

In a surprising turn of events in this new era of multiparty democracy where the public could finally stand up for its beliefs, we had a brief visit from the Principal Secretary in the Division of the Environment.

"The minister was quite taken with your article; she would like to meet you at the site tomorrow."

"Does she want to see the birds?" I asked, thinking about when it would be high tide and the birds would be there.

"No, I think she understands what you have said and admires your initiative."

We met the following day on the rough construction road across the reclaimed land. Danielle de St. Jorre was someone we had known for almost twenty years but whose elevation to a ministerial position had put an invisible barrier between us. She was, however, very friendly and pleased that we represented an opportunity for the government to engage with members of the public in an environment initiative.

"There are plans for this area and we expect to have the survey department down here in a month or two. Show me which part of the land is good for the birds and we will have it surveyed."

We talked briefly about the size of the land and pointed out a rough boundary. Before she left, the minister said, "We can't do this on a personal level, you will have to form an organisation to run what will be a privately-run bird sanctuary."

It wasn't difficult to find a dozen like-minded long-term residents willing to come together to create the Nature Protection Trust of Seychelles (NPTS). It proved only marginally more difficult to persuade the American Embassy to fund the fencing materials, Seychelles Breweries and Mr. Patel, the builder, to fund and build the hides. The Division of Environment chipped in to provide the sign board which carried their name and ours.

With our initially happy bunch of volunteers we planted a hedge of scaevola, a bushy beach-crest plant, along the car park fence. We mistakenly extended a small patch of bulrushes to create cover for the birds. What we really created was a source of back-breaking work cutting and clearing the bulrushes in subsequent years.

The oldest and busiest member of our Trust was Betty Beckett who was excused from doing physical chores in the slowly evolving muddy bird sanctuary. She was the leading natural history guide in Seychelles and liked nothing better than to share her contacts with her friends.

It was through Betty that we met David Stoddart who was an important member of the Seychelles Islands Foundation, the body that managed the World Heritage site of Aldabra atoll. David and Malcolm Coe, another Aldabra trustee and coincidentally Justin's supervisor at Oxford, proposed that I became one of the few non-government trustees on the SIF board.

A decision had been taken by SIF to renovate or possibly even rebuild the dilapidated Royal Society research station on Aldabra. As the only trustee with engineering experience, it fell to me to oversee the construction of the new station. An inspection visit to the Atoll was arranged on which I was to accompany several trustees to decide on how to rebuild the station while creating the minimum disturbance to the environment.

We were sitting at the domestic air terminal waiting for the aircraft to be fuelled prior to taking us to Assumption island, when we were informed that there would be a slight delay. This was at the time of the war in Rwanda and the stage-whispered morsels of conversation implied that some of our passengers had gone off to deal with an aircraft that was taking a shipment of confiscated arms to Goma in the Congo.

Flying in a small aircraft on the way to Assumption was a strange, almost dream-like experience. The towering cumulus clouds were well spaced apart, substantial to look at but quite ethereal as we disappeared into their enveloping silence, losing sight of the occasional tiny island in the dark blue sea below. As we made our approach to the island, we could see the two huge sand dunes that dominated this otherwise totally flat coral island. The scrubby landscape had once held important guano deposits but the mining operations had displaced the millions of seabirds that had nested there. Assumption was now the dropping-off point for visitors to Aldabra. The runway was in good order but the tiny settlement somewhat run down, overshadowed by the abandoned buildings and rusting machinery dating back to the time of the guano mining operations.

We boarded the Lady Geneviève, one of the island supply boats, for the crossing to Aldabra. The master of the vessel stood down and gave the wheel to his boss, the head of IDC. We must have been about midway between the islands when my fascination with the red-footed boobies, flying alongside the vessel hunting flying fish, was disrupted as the wind whipped my wide-brimmed Spanish straw hat off and sent it spinning down onto the surface of the sea. Almost immediately the boat began to go about.

"You don't need to worry about my hat" I shouted. "Let's leave it. It's not valuable!"

"No trouble", he said. "It'll only take a few minutes."

My hat was scooped up from its almost watery grave and brought up to the bridge. I went to thank him and was surprised to find him polite and courteous, not at all like his rumoured unpleasant and abrasive image. We got to talking about Silhouette and the discoveries made by the Oxford University expedition.

"Silhouette is really the last vestige of nature as it used to be on the granite islands", I suggested. "It really needs some formal protection".

"I don't know anything about conservation", he said. "If you would like to take on the responsibility I will make a house available for you, so that you can look after the conservation of the island."

Discussing this idea later in the day, he reminded me that firstly I would have to submit an outline management plan to the Department of Environment for their approval and he would then give his assent. Fortunately I had been involved in writing part of the management plan for Aldabra, so that when Justin and I set to work on the Silhouette Conservation Project plan, we already understood what was required.

Getting the plans accepted necessitated negotiations that took time and patience. While we were thus occupied, we made two day trips to Silhouette. The first was with Mike Maunder who was from Kew, although representing Fauna & Flora International, to give him some idea of our ambitious plans. He advised us on the type and form of agreement we should make with the owner of the island. This was drawn up by a lawyer friend, Bernard Georges, so that we would have a legally binding agreement. Unfortunately, as it was to prove later, when we submitted the agreement for signing, it only travelled as far as the waste paper bin in the legal department and was never seen again. We, who were always too busy, were also too trusting to insist.

My second trip was an opportunity to take David Stoddart to Silhouette, an island he had not previously visited. We made a brief tour of the settlement before spending time inspecting all the historical remains of the Dauban family. Pat Matyot was on the island at the time and as David was not inclined to scramble up through the vegetation and rocks, Pat accompanied me to the jumble of gigantic boulders that provided shelter for a small group of highly endangered sheath-tailed bats.

As it turned out, it was as well that David had not joined our expedition. The climb through the forest started across several large, slippery, sloping rocks and then fortunately evolved into a narrow, seldom-used steep trail. On a narrow, almost level contour, we came to a jumble of huge granite boulders so large that they towered above the surrounding forest.

Piled as they were, one on top of the other, the rocks formed cave-like openings, some with almost horizontal ceilings. A little out breath and as quietly as possible, we approached one of the openings where the bats were known to roost. There were six small pipistrelle-sized bats clinging to the roof quite close to each other and slightly fidgety. We watched them for a while, listening to their chittery conversations, until one left its place and started to fly around inside the roost - it was time for us to leave.

In anticipation of our move to Silhouette, we had given up our rented flat at St. Louis and taken up temporary residence in our studio at Beau Vallon. However, the months of waiting dragged on. Our state of limbo, stuck in the cramped "temporary" accommodation became a subject for much friendly banter. Each time we accepted a proposal for our new quarters on Silhouette, a reason was found to cancel the arrangement. At one stage we went so far as to suggest that we import a prefabricated timber log house from South Africa, but that was wrought with legal difficulties. We were unaware that there was absolutely no private land tenure on Silhouette.

And then, much to our relief, we were informed in April 1997, that a suitable building had become available and that we should prepare ourselves to make the move in early May.

CHAPTER THREE

The calm doldrums sea, reflecting an almost cloudless sky, heralded an auspicious start to the journey to our new lives on Silhouette. As the "Lady Geneviève" made steady progress towards the island, an occasional startled flying fish sped away from her bows, leaving a long dotted line on the sea surface which ended in a splashed full stop. Small flocks of noddy terns beat their way purposefully above their reflections. Silent shearwaters on motionless wings banked and turned as they inspected our disturbed wake.

A short distance from the old stone jetty but still in the deep water beyond the reef, she dropped her anchor. We waited for the fibre-glass pirogue to come alongside in preparation for dismbarking the passengers. In a gesture more to do with politesse than machismo, the men and children clambered down the vertical ladder and took an insecure step out to the pirogue, while the ladies and our two dachshunds were seated in a small landing craft that was lifted by the ship's crane and lowered onto the sea. Once we were all ashore, the serious business of unloading the supplies and our belongings got underway.

At the landward end of the old stone jetty, overlooked by the Grande Case, an unremarkable building housed the island manager's office and the store room. Behind the stores was an old house where the Dubignon family lived and across the sandy road from them, a ramshackle rusting building housed the calorifer where the copra was dried. Fifty metres further on we found the house that had been allocated to our project. It was a relatively new building, probably about ten years old. It had three reasonably sized bedrooms, a bathroom, kitchen and sitting room. The floors were unadorned bare grey concrete and the walls in desperate need of a coat or two of new paint. The corrugated iron roof was showing the first blush of rust, occasioned by the close proximity of the sea. Nevertheless, we thought it a big improvement on the cramped quarters in the back of our studio on Beau Vallon beach.

Diagonally across the sandy track from the house, on the beachside, and partly shaded by a line of *Tabebuia* trees, were the foundations and broken fragments of the floor of a house; a reminder of previous inhabitants of this end of La Passe. Standing in regal solitude was an unblemished white porecein toilet pedestal securely cemented to the concrete floor, providing, perhaps, somewhere from which to contemplate the forgotten purple bougainvillea struggling through the fractured floor.

At the far end of the line of trees, tucked into the last few metres of flat land before the steep rocky headland, was a traditional wooden creole house on stone plinths. An elderly lady, her son and several feral chickens lived there.

Behind our new abode lay a small, sometimes tidal, marsh which we named "the Dauban Marsh". Beyond the house, bordered on one side by the track and the line of trees and on the other side by the marsh, was an open field. At the far end of the field, near the old lady's wooden house, stood a derelict building with substantial coral and red-earth walls. The roof, long rusted through, was supported on a skeleton of rough-hewn hardwood beams. A partially collapsed lean-to on the marsh side of the building and a separate corrugated iron kitchen building were all that remained of what had once been home for the Dubignon family. They had been the last residents of the Anse Lascars settlement before it was abandoned and the inhabitants moved to La Passe where there was a permanent water supply and the magic of electricity. In recent times, the Dubignons had been moved into the more spacious and marginally less derelict building opposite the calorifer.

Jimmy, the island manager, who lived in a spacious wooden house on the other side of the Grande Case, arrived on the island's only tractor towing a battered trailer loaded with our boxes and furniture. He was very pleasant, gave us the keys to the house and his men proceeded to move all our belongings into the sitting room. Jimmy said he would send his electrician the next day to connect our electric cooker and attend to anything else that needed attention.

There were around 150 people living on Silhouette at the time. Of these, only eight or nine lived on the other side of the island at Grande Barbe, one couple lived in the isolated bay of Anse Mondon and everyone else lived at La Passe, the village on this side of the island. With the exception of the few ladies who were employed at the Lodge, everyone else, men and women, were employed by the owner. We had lived in Seychelles for 27 years and were fully aware of the feudal system under which the islands were managed, but even so, it came as a bit of a shock to find ourselves part of it. The owner's company, which managed all the outer islands and Silhouette, owned the islands in their entirety. All the workers resident on the islands, including even those who were born there, were employed on twelve-month contracts and had no property rights. The only shop was the company shop, which deducted the cost of the workers' purchases directly from their salaries. At the end of each twelve-month contract the worker returned to Mahé and was paid the wages he had earned over this period, less deductions for his purchases in the shop. He then had a short holiday and applied to renew his contract for another year. If approved, he then returned to the island.

As on the Chagos Islands, this feudal system persisted all through the heyday of the copra industry; contract workers meant no land rights. The only advantage in this paternalistic system was that the workers paid no rent and water and electricity were free. This archaic arrangement was a fact of life for people living on the islands; something they accepted as quite normal.

There was a considerable amount of work to be done to get the house up to scratch – but not on this first day. We settled our dogs, Max and Tekel, in the empty kitchen for the night and wandered through the village to the Silhouette Island Lodge. We were booked in for three nights in anticipation of working all day and enjoying the luxury of some-one else cooking our dinner and making the bed, and breakfast, for us. Ornella and her daughter Sabrina were very welcoming and eased us gently into this somewhat strange island life.

For three days we beavered away at painting the interior of the house, arranging the furniture and unpacking our boxes. We decided to use the bedroom nearest the sitting room as our conservation centre, laboratory and office. We used the large cupboard that contained our craftwork as a divider between the sitting room and dining area. The plan was to use this as a sales point for our craft work which, when added to the income from our studio on Beau Vallon, would keep the wolf from the door while we concentrated on our conservation projects.

On our first night in our new abode we ate our evening meal listening to the gentle whisper of the sea as the tide flooded across the reef. We read awhile then put the dogs to bed in the kitchen and crept into our welcoming bed and straight into the arms of Morpheus. Ah! Bliss!

The night was so still and calm.

Around midnight we were both woken by a sudden bright light flashing across the wooden shutters. A torch? No. Too bright. Ten seconds later there came a deep rumble of distant thunder. The flashes of lightning soon became more frequent; the thunder building up in intensity until both lightning and thunder fused into one huge electrical storm, reaching a crescendo that cracked and roared as it echoed off the mountains. The dogs, needing assurance that the world had not ended, were scratching frantically at the kitchen door and were given shelter under our bed. And then as the thunder lost its menacing force, the rain began to roar down onto our tin roof. Gill lay awake listening to the rain, the dogs settled down and I returned to my dormant state, knowing we were safe and secure and most important of all, dry.

The sun rose on a beautiful clear morning, the grass and the leaves shimmering in the bright sunlight. The faintest promise of the south-east tradewind stirred in the topmost branches of the trees. We ventured out into this rain-refreshed morning, the household chores now behind us, and began to think about our first big conservation project. This was to be a captive breeding centre for which Justin had raised the funds, enabling us to purchase eight giant tortoises. The Seychelles Giant Tortoise Conservation Project was based on research undertaken by Justin and his wife Laura, which had identified several tortoises that were not the more common Aldabra tortoises but were, in all likelihood, survivors of the giant tortoises native to these granite islands. Our contribution was to prepare for the arrival of the animals and make sure they would be housed and cared for in the best possible conditions.

The land between the house and the derelict building about fifty metres away sloped gently down to the shoreline of the marsh and was an obvious choice for the tortoise enclosures. We were relieved that there were no objections to our using this open space, the only problem being to fence the area securely.

Getting help with the building of the fence should not have been a problem as during the negotiations prior to our move to Silhouette it had been suggested that two or three men would be made available to assist with our conservation work. When I asked Jimmy for some men to help with the task of cutting the many fenceposts we would need, it was immediately obvious that he had not been told about any such arrangement. He seemed reticent about offering any help without receiving official instructions.

When he came by the day after my request, I had started digging the post holes in the sandy soil. He was alone – no helpers in sight.

"The holes need to be quite deep so that the posts cannot be pushed over", I said to him.

"And close together", he suggested. He stood watching me for a while, then said, "Let me speak to Justin Moustache before you do any more work."

Justin Moustache was the general manager, a conscientious and very pleasant young man to whom I had spoken biefly on several occasions at the head office. Towards the end of the working day, Jimmy's tractor came grumbling down the road, towing the trailer which was full of timber. It was nearly four o'clock and his men off-loaded the timber, piled back into the trailer and set off for home.

When asked where the timber came from, Jimmy informed me that it was "from the farm". The farm was at the far end of the village, beyond the marsh that curled around the Lodge. It consisted of several enormous poultry barns where they had raised day-old chicks that were flown in from Holland every few weeks. When we had first seen these impressive buildings at the time of the Oxford expedition, they were relatively new, built maybe four or five years earlier.

Jimmy and his men had returned to the farm for still more timber the next day when we went along to see exactly where this valuable source of timber was. The huge poultry farm now lay abandoned, even the pig-sty at the far end of the farm was empty. The only functioning barn contained a couple of tired-looking cows. Most of the roof-sheeting had been removed from the poultry hangars, leaving the roof timbers exposed to the elements. The rafters and beams were now being recycled to build our tortoise enclosures.

On the way back we stopped at the Lodge to ask Ornella about the farm.

"It had to go", she offered at the end of a big resigned Italianate shrug. "The smell of all the chicken caca; the feathers and bits of chicken all over the beach! My God! It was not possible to run the hotel and have a chicken farm next door!"

This seemed at the time to be a perfectly acceptable explanation; a choice between earning money from the poultry farm, or obtaining money from the lease of the hotel property. I wondered if, as with many overseas–funded projects, once the seed money was spent and the difficulty of making ends meet became a problem, the whole enterprise had fallen apart.

However, we were more thankful than concerned about this unexpected source of timber and grateful that in their spare time Jimmy's men began to construct the first enclosure. Our initial plan was to have two enclosures each about 30 metres wide and taking up the 50 metres between the road and the marsh edge. Over the next two weeks as the enclosures slowly began to take shape, we cleared up some of the visible rubbish from what must have been the village garbage dump for some years. Almost every piece of sacking protruding from the sand revealed, when unearthed, bottles, tins, plastic bags and boxes, bits of metal, broken crockery and even some perfectly good cutlery.

The marsh itself had not escaped the disregard that people have for their natural surroundings. Some weeks later when the dry south-easterly winds and the relentless sun had evaporated the marsh, reducing it to two narrow pools seething with what remained of the fish population, I spent several days treading carefully over the sun-baked mud, collecting all the discarded rubbish. Until then, humanity's usual detritus of yet more plastic, glass and metal had been lying invisible below the surface of the water. A half-buried tractor tyre and an engine attached to a metal chassis were too difficult to move and were left as enduring symbols of machinery overcoming Nature.

On the final day of my clean up, I sat down on the edge of the culvert where the marsh sneaked under the road on its way to the sea. A grey heron was stalking around the trapped fish, deciding which one looked the tastiest. A little mudskipper came flicking out of the water under the bridge, his bulbous eyes seemed to swivel about as he took in the view across the newly tidied-up marsh. We were probably both thinking what a beautiful place this must have been before it became a rubbish tip.

Work on the enclosure proceeded at a steady pace. Towards the end of July when Justin and I set off for Mahé to collect the tortoises, we left Gill, Laura and baby Oliver to keep an eye on the final days of enclosure construction. Three frantic days later we returned to Silhouette with our cargo of eight giant tortoises. Jimmy and his men were there to ferry the tortoises ashore and transfer them to their brand new enclosure.

We started the tortoise project with a clean slate, knowing that the animals needed to be cared for in better conditions than those that generally prevailed in Seychelles. We were also not in a position to keep them in the exotic conditions we had seen at the Charles Darwin Station on Galapagos some years previously, where generous financial sponsorship permitted them to build stone-walled enclosures with elevated board-walks and sun-shaded seating. As there was no relevant literature on tortoise husbandry in their natural surroundings, we collected a wide variety of native and introduced plants in order to determine their dietary preferences – no longer a diet of the hotel kitchen waste they had eaten in their previous lives.

When Justin and Laura returned to Cambridge, half of their luggage allowance was taken up by dried leaves and plants which were to be analysed for their suitability as healthy tortoise food. Left to my own devices, the enormity of the task of collecting great bundles of food for the tortoises each day soon became apparent. On alternate days I cut the long streamers of beach morning glory and the abundant creepers in the lowland forest.

Each day we rose with the sun, let the dogs out, ate our breakfast and attended to the tortoises, collecting their food, cleaning out the previous day's remains and the manure. The dogs soon lost interest in the tortoises because they would not respond, smelt a bit odd and even their sweet-potato-shaped manure smelled boringly of vegetation. No thoroughbred chap would even bother to rub his dachsund's back on something that was so vegetably smelling! The dogs thought it better that I disposed of the manure.

The Seychelles Giant Tortoise Conservation Project was not the only reason we were on Silhouette. We had written a management plan based on our assumptions of what needed to be done to improve the environment and to protect the species that survived in the natural environment. All such activities depended on good solid groundwork and understanding of what we were conserving and how we could do so.

We ventured into areas of Silhouette that we were not familiar with, beginning to understand the terrain and making assessments of what needed doing. In those first few months we were not really properly equipped to undertake full investigations but as the only local non-government conservation organisation in Seychelles we found ourselves the beneficiaries of funding from both the American Embassy and the British High Commission. With their help we were able to furnish our office and acquire a replacement for our word processor – our first computer and printer. For good measure the American Embassy threw in a second-hand refrigerator for freezing biological specimens but which also had ample space for storing soft drinks and beer.

The High Commission provided the funds that enabled us to replace our tiny field microscope with two professional models, a compound and a binocular microscope. When they arrived, the High Commissioner decided to pay us a short visit to see what we had bought with the funds. Concerned that he might not understand that our office was too small to be a laboratory as well, we moved some of the furniture into the spare bedroom and put a trestle table in the "laboratory". We painted the top white, covered the trestles with a bedspread and arranged the microscope and all the petri dishes, specimens and herbarium collection on this pristine worktop. Fortunately he was quite happy with our primitive laboratory and the tortoise project. He offered further support in the next year's funding round.

The display on the temporary testle table made us realise that we were in need of a proper laboratory space, separate from our office. The old coral building at the far end of the second enclosure was a distinct, but probably expensive, possibility. The walls were very substantial and the concrete floor in reasonable condition. The lean-to at the back had a good solid floor which was large enough to accommodate the laboratory. There was even a secondary lean-to housing a toilet and shower, although the plumbing had long since rotted away.

The plans I drew up for the conversion of the building into an information centre and laboratory were approved on the understanding that we would provide the finance for all the necessary building work. We submitted the plans, and three expensive quotations from local builders, to the government's Environment Trust Fund. Unfortunately, as we had previously been recipients of funding for a research project on the native terrapins, they were not willing to fund the restoration of one of the oldest buildings on the island and we were obliged to put the plans back in the filing cabinet for the time being.

CHAPTER FOUR

The days were filled with beautiful warm tropical sunshine. The nights were balmy under an inky-black star-filled sky where the milky way was so intense it looked like a thin veil of cloud. These brought with them a feeling of peace and being privileged to find ourselves on this still primitive island. There were no tarred roads, only sandy tracks. There were no cars, nor motorbikes, not even bicycles; only one tractor.

While some of the inhabitants looked upon us as unwanted invaders from the big island, our immediate neighbours were welcoming. The elderly lady and her son in the old wooden house at the end of the beach, and the Dubignon family, James and May with their elder daughter, Margaret, and three younger children, were all considerate neighbours.

Like all Seychellois, they "kept" a nomadic flock of chickens, some mixed-up ducks and one lonely guinea-fowl that spent their days scratching in the leaf-litter under the trees. Max and Teckel Dachshund tried their best to protect us from these marauding birds by keeping half an eye open ready for the chase. We had to bury one or two scrawny catastrophies in case James came to look for them, but he probably didn't know how many chickens he had in any case. On moonlit nights when they couldn't sleep, the roosters were a bit of a pain, but then so were the argumentative gangs of fruit bats in the large Indian Almond tree that shaded our bedroom. In the fruiting season, it sometimes seemed as though the bats were deliberately dropping the fruit on our tin roof. Peace always came when the gentle rain fell at night and the chickens and the bats went home to bed.

As the months went by, civilisation came almost unnoticed to our desert island. Ours was but one of the many houses with an over-tall television aerial that provided somewhat wintery snow-filled reception. We had waited what seemed like ages to acquire a telephone line. When the underground cable had been installed and the connection made, we had only the third phone on Silhouette. The island manager had one, the second was on the hotel reception desk and ours, the third. Everyone else used the one and only public phone. The computer and the phone gave us, for the first time, access to e-mails and saved us a fortune on lengthy international calls to Justin.

Computers with their mysteriously intricate working and self-opinionated attitude were not designed to live in this salt-laden atmosphere. We were obliged to invest in an air-conditioner for the office and took advantage of it by installing a second fan unit in our bedroom. The air conditioner made its own demands; it wasn't going to work in an office with wooden shutters and no glass in the window. Charles, at the aluminium window workshop on Mahé, kindly donated two large sheets of unsellable mirror glass for our office window.

This proved to be a very disturbing experience for the mynah birds who found that they could not get hold of the feathers of these impenetrable reflected birds. They pecked, squawked and threatened these apparitions and even tried bowing politely, all to no avail. A little male Seychelles sunbird also met his match but after a few days of fluttering up and down the window panes, decided there wasn't much point. There were one or two heart-stopping moments when the turtledoves ventured with a resounding thump into the new landscape reflected in the window.

It was as well that the then solitary grey heron who frequented the marsh never took a shortcut through our window on his frequent visits to the reef flats. Grey herons, like the black-crowned night herons, were fairly recent re-colonisers of the islands after a long absence. In the later afternoons we often saw a pair of night herons stalking through the shallows of the marsh, their bright red eyes glowing like embers, staring intensely into the water.

One night in March 1998 the waves were crashing over the reef, driven to a frenzy by the north-westerly wind that ripped the dry fronds from the coconut palms and sent them crashing to the ground. The night herons took fright and came "wokking" past the house on their way to somewhere safe. Quite suddenly through the noise of the wind came an ever-increasing cacophony of seabird calls. In the brief moments of moonlight, glimpsed through the scudding clouds, we saw thousands of what we thought were brown noddy terns, flying downwind. This night-time avian chaos was something we had never seen before.

The following morning, the persistent wind and the dark storm clouds were still rushing across the sky. Somewhere close by we could still hear the noddies calling at full pitch. We scrambled up the steep rough path that leads to Anse Cimetière where a small flat area of land facing Mahé had once served as the workers' cemetery. The noddies' constant calls filled the air as they flew in and out of the casuarina trees that covered most of the headland.

We estimated that there may have been five thousand birds on the headland where they roosted for almost a month. Then, just as suddenly as they had come, they disappeared. James Dubignon told me that over the many years he had lived on Silhouette he recalled only very occasional seasonal invasions like this. Our hopes that the island would join the ranks of the other seabird reserves dashed, we returned to our more pressing chores of tortoise and terrapin husbandry. We had established a captive breeding project for the two species of terrapin that were found in Seychelles. They were housed in plastic lined ponds that lay between the house and the tortoise enclosures. With the approval of the Ministry of Environment we had embarked on this project with the intention of understanding and improving the conservation needs of the terrapins.

The not infrequent meetings on Mahé with the Ministry, the company, SIF and work on the bird sanctuary were only possible when Bluefin, a game fishing boat, was chartered to run a twice weekly service to Silhouette. This new service was reasonably priced but as the trips started on Mahé and returned there after only a brief stop on the island, I (and sometimes, we) had to spend two or three nights camped in the back of the Beau Vallon studio.

Commuting to the main island, for that is what it felt like, and staying over those few nights became less tedious when Ornella decided that our presence on Silhouette was a tourism asset and offered us staff rates on any spare seats on the helicopter service that ferried her guests to and from the island.

Prior to this new arrangement with the helicopter, I had been asked to attend a meeting on Mahé and was obliged to stay there for the full three days waiting for the next Bluefin trip home. On my return Gill was eager to tell me that she had found two guests from the Lodge admiring the tortoises. They had shown a more than casual interest in what we were doing, not only our work with the tortoises and terrapins, but also the conservation work we were embarking upon. They were invited into the house where the seating was more comfortable and while his English lady partner looked at our displays, this sympathetic Dutch gentleman continued his questions about our aims.

"If you had the money, what would be your first priority?" he asked.

"We would really like to convert those old buildings in the tortoise enclosure into an information centre and laboratory", Gill told him.

"Have you any idea of the cost?"

"We already have a set of plans and an estimated budget of about $25,000; that's our dream."

We didn't know at the time, but Paul van Vlissingen was a wealthy industrialist and was later reputed to be the richest man in Scotland and the largest foreign landowner in the United Kingdom. He was a member of the Prince Bernard Nature Trust on whose behalf he sent us a fax a week later, offering to pay for the building work. The owner had no objections to the conversion as long as he was not expected to fork out any money. He made an important contribution by transporting all the building materials on the monthly supply boat.

The information centre slowly took shape over several months with help from three members of the island staff in their after-work hours.

CHAPTER FIVE

There is no lingering twilight on the equator. Sunset, however spectacular, is a very brief affair between the bright light of late afternoon and the sudden darkness as the sea absorbs the sun. The two hours of that late afternoon sunshine between four, when the men's formal working hours ended, and six, when the sun set, we devoted to building the information centre.

In the first years of our time on Silhouette, the workers were employed to keep the island tidy and sometimes to harvest coconuts and cinnamon bark. The demand for these two agricultural crops was sporadic and appeared to be in response to specific orders. Coconuts were collected from easily accessible areas around the Lodge and along the shoreline. The nuts were dehusked and split in

two, then laid out to dry on a large concrete pad outside the Dubignon's house. Some days later, the partially dried flesh, the copra, was eased out of the shells and placed on drying racks in the calorifer building where the heat from a permanent fire dried the copra in readiness for bagging and export.

(Photo: G.van Heygen)

The romantic image of coconut palms leaning over pale sandy tropical beaches and their wind-ruffled fronds standing tall in the lush lowland forests were a reminder of their historical importance to the economy of the islands. Now, forgotten and unwanted, the mature nuts fell in ever mounting heaps on the forest floor. The sprouting fertile progeny of these elegant palms spread across the uneven ground in their own struggle for survival, smothering the natural vegetation.

Cinnamon, spread as it was by the birds into the heart of the forests, was an even worse conservation nightmare. The tradition was to fell trees of a certain size, usually severing them at about waist height, then removing the bark from the trunk and large limbs. The bark was brought down and spread out to dry in the sun on the same concrete pad.

In days gone by, the remains of the felled trees had been used as fuel in the calorifer, but were now left where they fell, destroying any plants that had managed to survive in the dense shade the trees had provided. Cinnamon leaf litter had a toxic effect on all but the hardiest of plants and in an act of sabotage equal to that of the coconuts, cinnamon trees littered the forest floor with a multitude of sprouting seeds.

We inadvertently discovered another introduced alien agricultural crop that had completely taken over one of the most important high altitude habitats at Mare aux Cochons – coffee. At some time in the final years of Henri Dauban's struggle to find employment for his workers, he had decided to grow coffee. The marshy plateau at Mare aux Cochons provided a milder damper climate than at sea level. He had the marsh channelled and partially drained, then planted it with coffee seedlings. A small building to house someone to oversee the plantation was built but the strenuous climb up from the settlement and the isolation soon led to its being abandoned. Like cinnamon, coffee produces an abundance of seeds that germinate readily and turned what had once been an area of biodiversity abundance into an all but impenetrable jungle of coffee plants.

Mare aux Cochons had provided biologist Hugh Scott with a treasure trove of invertebrate specimens during the 1905 Percy Sladen Trust Expeditions. Knowing this, when Justin and I investigated the area, we thought we could get help from island workers to rehabilitate a reasonable portion of the marsh and raise the funds for the work by establishing a two-day hiking trail around the island, with an overnight camp using the abandoned building. Help with this project was not forthcoming as the workers were always otherwise employed and we and our members were unable to sustain a project in such a remote area.

We made a second attempt by including the rehabilitation of Mare aux Cochons in the "Forest Conservation on Silhouette" proposal we developed with the Forestry Department and which was approved by the owner. This proposal was submitted for World Bank funding under their Global Environment Fund (GEF). The lead consultant from the International Union for the Conservation of Nature,

IUCN, and a senior representative from the World Bank came to Silhouette to look at the feasibility of our project. They were very enthusiastic and left us thinking that it was a distinct possibility. However, the Ministry of Environment persuaded the World Bank to restructure the proposal into a public sector management and data gathering exercise which removed all mention of the protection of Silhouette's forests and any actual conservation action from the GEF project.

While the island workers were employed with harvesting their coconuts and cinnamon, we embarked on a two-man, and sometimes one man, one woman pilot project aimed at restoring some of the habitat destruction. We started clearing dense growths of coconut scrub and the carpets of cinnamon seedlings so that we could reintroduce the native plants and endemic trees. We were intent on creating a lowland forest trail from the Dauban mausoleum to the top of the Anse Lascars track. It would provide a short and easy hike through interesting natural forest vegetation for the increasing number of day visitors and those guests from the Lodge who were unable to join our excursions into the high forests at Jardin Marron.

The number of day trips from Mahé steadily increased as the tour operators became aware that they could rely on a warm welcome and an interesting tour of the Grande Case, an informative visit to the tortoises and the Dauban Mausoleum. We received a token payment for each group, irrespective of the number of visitors but raised funds for our conservation projects through the sale of T-shirts and souvenirs. We thought, rather naively, that attracting these excursions.

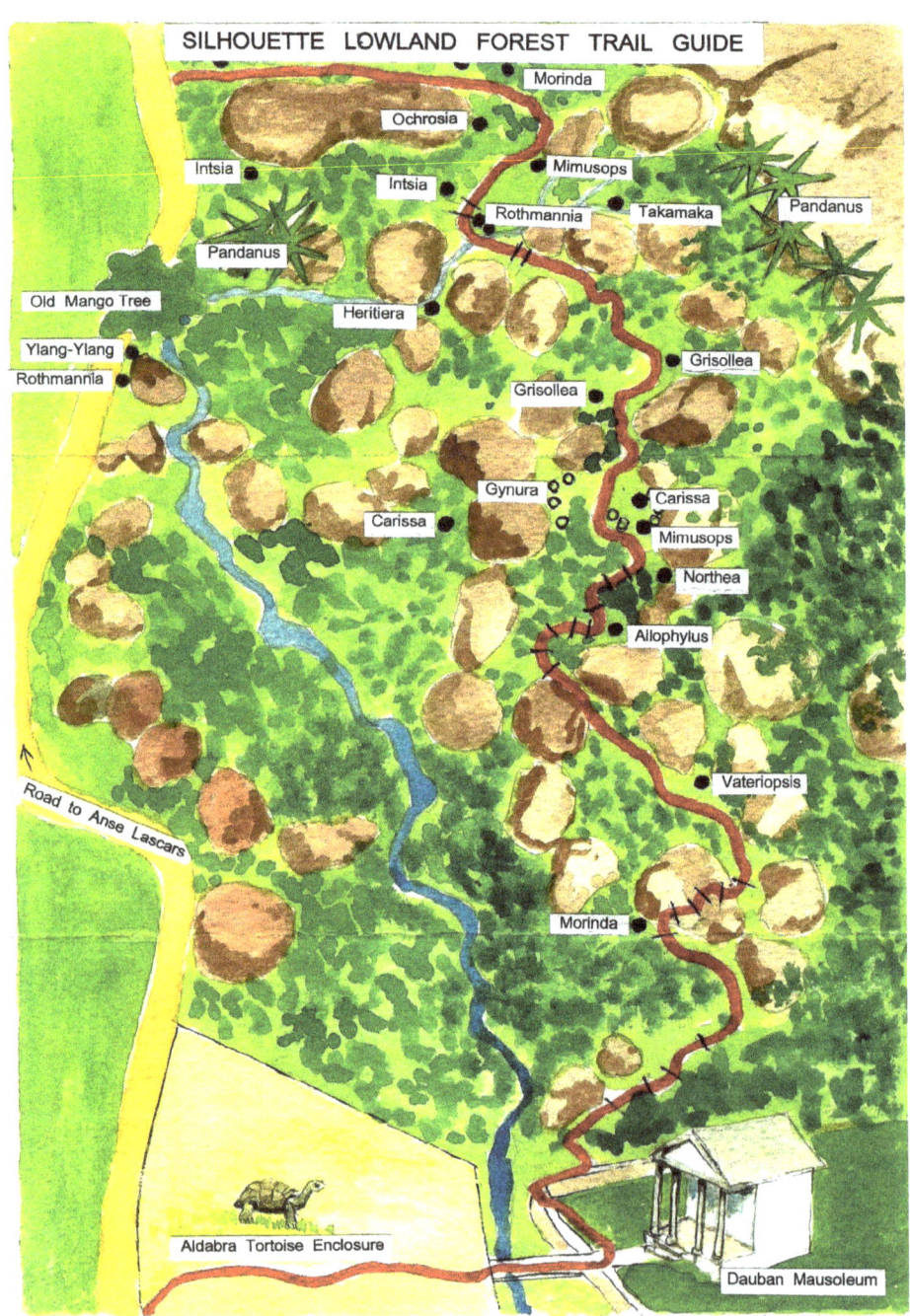

to Silhouette for which the owner charged a landing fee for each visitor, was our way of contributing to the island's income so that we were a benefit and not a burden to him.

The following year we were lucky to have a Belgian herpetologist, Guy van Heygen, who, through his son, Emmanuel, who worked with the animal food supplier Exoterra, arranged sponsorship of all the terrapin equipment and food we ever needed. Guy spent much of his time studying geckos and chameleons in the forest, as well as fulfilling his tortoise-sitting duties. He became a regular volunteer, returning a number of times in subsequent years.

In mid-1999 colleagues from Aride island, Frankie Hobro and Daryl Birch, stepped into our shoes. Beyond the call of normal duties they also mounted an exhibition of our craftwork at the local craft fair held in the Grande Case. At the end of that year, Ann and Bill Truscott took over our duties and like Guy van Heygen became regular volunteers.

A month before Ann and Bill arrived, we had completed work on the information centre and laboratory. Among the fifty people who attended the formal opening were members of our Trust, the island manager and staff, including my part-time building companions, the local press and television station and a group of eleven ladies and one gentleman who were tortoise specialists and enthusiasts from the British Chelonia Group and sponsors of some of our tortoises.

The new facilities provided us with a large space in which to display information about all aspects of nature on the island and a shop space to raise funds. The air conditioned room also housed the storage and display cabinets for our growing scientific collection. The laboratory was light and airy and intended not only for our own use, but also as a facility available for visiting scientists.

(Photo: G.van Heygen)

The volunteers who came from 2000 onwards were often less involved in our tortoise project and more likely to be occupied with data collection and monitoring in the forest. Lala Gregorek and Richard Pitman were involved in all aspects of our projects and when we took a short break Lala looked after the house and Teckel for us – Max had succumbed to an overdose of heartworm a while back and now lay peacefully beneath a spreading frangipani tree in the garden. Richard made some superb drawings of the tortoises and did some collecting of his own when he persuaded Margaret Dubignon to become part of his life in England.

When Johanna Willi came in July, she spent most of her time collecting invertebrates in the forest with Justin. On one of these collecting days she brought the crown of a *Dracaena* plant down to the laboratory where she could dismantle it leaf by leaf to see what lived in the leaf axils. Much to her surprise and pleasure, one of the hidden secrets turned out to be not an insect, but a minute frog.

These tiny endemic sooglossid frogs, a mere ten millimetres long, are distantly related to a species of small Indian toads and like toads they are not necessarily associated with water, being instead inhabitants of the damp forest floor leaf litter. Gardiner's frog, the smallest of the species, has the unusual ability for a frog of laying eggs from which fully formed baby frogs emerge having bypassed the tadpole stage. The slightly larger Seychelles frog, on the other hand, is like a midwife toad in that once the tadpoles have hatched they are carried on the back of the adult until they metamorphose into froglets.

This little frog, hidden in Johanna's plant was unmistakably a sooglossid frog but on close scrutiny did not conform to the characteristics of the other two sooglossids. It was later described as a new species – the Seychelles palm frog, because many of the subsequent specimens were found hidden in the axils of endemic spiny palms.

Johanna was the first of the volunteers to work with Justin on a new research project that had received only reluctant support from the Ministry of Environment. This project was building on the data that Justin had compiled when he produced the first entire species list for Silhouette in 1998. The new project, the Indian Ocean Biodiversity Assessment 2000-2005, set out to extend and update the Percy Sladen Trust Expeditions a century earlier. The assessment would collect, identify and catalogue biological specimens from every island in the Seychelles archipelago. Silhouette was the obvious starting point as we had the laboratory facilities and could standardise and refine the collecting method and preserve the specimens for identification through a network of specialist taxonomists with whom Justin had made contact.

When the specimens, samples and data for Silhouette had been assembled, Justin and various colleagues moved on to the other islands. In the forest at Jardin Marrons he had left a malaise trap that was designed to catch mainly flying insects. It was my responsibility over the next twelve months to change the collecting bottles on the trap. I did this once every fortnight on one of my frequent hiking excursions with guests from the Lodge.

The extra demands made on our time were noticed by Justin Moustache who knew that he was not permitted to allocate any staff to our projects.

"You really need some help, don't you?" he asked.

"We try our best not to make too many demands of Jimmy and his men, but I am tempted some days", I told him.

"Tell you what I'll do", he said, "but you are not to say anything to my boss, O.K?"

"Tell me."

"The new tractor driver, Jules, seems like a good man. He can help you but only when he is not needed elsewhere."

I could have kissed him, but I didn't. Jules had already been a help by bringing loads of tortoise food when the men were cutting vegetation along the beach-crest. He would prove to be a very willing and enthusiastic part-time assistant.

Halfway through my chat with Justin Moustache I noticed, out of the corner of my eye, a large landing craft approaching the pass through the reef. It was high tide and this flat-bottomed vessel came onto the reef flat next to the jetty and unloaded the largest excavator I had ever seen. In the days that followed, it became obvious that the excavator was digging something far more ambitious than a simple channel alongside the jetty. It set about excavating a large square basin in the reef to a depth of six metres. When it finished its clanking, grinding, squealing task there were two mountains of spoil, one on each side of the basin, and the approach channel that had always been a narrow pass was now suitable for quite large vessels.

Some months earlier I had been asked to write an Environment Impact Assessment for the owner to submit to the planning division. It was a study of the marine life on the tidal flats adjacent to the old stone jetty where I was told a channel would be excavated to allow access by larger vessels at low tide.

The EIA I had written had obviously been an exercise in bureaucratic formality. It looked as if this excessive expansion to the approach and landing stage on Silhouette was intended for something more serious than landing a few tourist boats.

CHAPTER SIX

In that brief interlude between afternoon and night when the sun, sky and sea were still glowing red, James strolled along the jetty, deep in thought, as he had done on many occasions in the past. His solitary figure silhouetted against the sunset as he stood on the end of the jetty had been our point of focus, but on this evening his lonely vigil was absorbed into the background of towering heaps of dredged up sand and coral that blocked out the view of the sea and of North Island beyond. Poor James, what must have been on your mind as you stood there dreaming on the end of the Daubans' old stone jetty?

The bulldozer arrived the next day, spreading the heaps of excavated material up against the jetty, absorbing it into the two embracing arms of the new harbour. When it was all level and compacted, the exposed edges were swathed in a black screening fabric to prevent the sand from leaching out. Boat-loads of granite rocks from Mahé were dumped over the fabric as protection against the wind and waves. The imported rocks protected the landscape on Silhouette from the desecration of major blasting and transport operations.

Some months earlier, the Dubignon family had been moved to a new, marginally more modern, house in the village. Their vacant house opposite the calorifer now housed a team of imported Indian builders who had become our nearest neighbours when they moved in. They were employed to construct a concrete landing stage in the harbour. This at least made getting on and off the island a much less hazardous adventure. Ah! Such were the benefits of civilisation. But, as always, development comes at a cost to the natural environment.

Lying in the shallow pools on the reef flat at low tide, we found hundreds, if not thousands of dead sea cucumbers of several different species, brittle stars, crabs and other small reef-flat animals. Seashells were to be found everywhere in quite unimaginable quantities. The extent of the damage to this relatively small area of reef flat was quite astounding.

We took the opportunity that the destruction brought to sample the range of sea shells brought up from the reef. It took us many months of slow, eye-straining perusal of the available and often confusing descriptive literature to identify and classify some 356 different shells. Considering the brutality of the machinery that had excavated and bulldozed the sand and coral, we were surprised to find so many perfect, undamaged empty shells.

On the positive side, there were those marine species eager to take advantage of the new calm harbour basin: shoals of small striped scissor-tail fish, silvery sap-sap fish, glistening like sunlit diamonds and grey mullet playing follow-my leader, their upturned mouths skimming the surface of the sea as though gulping for air. Most exciting of all was a large hammer-head shark that made a

slow circuit of the harbour with slow purposeful strokes of its tail, inspecting this deconstructed piece of reef. The fishermen were there too, only minutes after their normal working hours, but it wasn't until the shark made the mistake of a second tour of inspection that they succeeded in catching it.

The black screen-cloth that had been used along the harbour walls would, I thought, be a big improvement on the very inadequate shade cloth I had used on the new terrapin enclosure we had built with funds from the American Embassy. When I asked about the supplier, I was directed to someone I knew in the government. It transpired that he was the sole importer who sold it on to the government for all its reclamation projects. My request to purchase enough for our needs represented a mere off-cut and we were grateful to receive it as a donation to the terrapin project.

The new terrapin enclosures, shaded with this denser shade cloth, had been in use for only a few weeks when I was surprised to find Mme. Dubignon and her two grandsons on the doorstep. Roger, the elder of the two, stretched his arms out indicating something clasped between his palms.

"What's this?" I asked.

He moved his thumbs apart and turned his hands so that I could see a small bright staring eye.

"Soupape!" – the Creole word for terrapin.

"Where did you find it?" in my best frenchified Creole.

"At the farm", from Mme. Dubignon, answering on his behalf as the terrapin tried to prise itself from Roger's grasp.

Apparently this small juvenile yellow-bellied terrapin, for that is what it proved to be, had wandered out of the overgrown stream that ran behind the abandoned farm and fed into the marsh at the Lodge. Roger and his brother, Gino, had found it scuttling along the path in the direction of the derelict poultry barns. They decided it would be safer in the company of the other juvenile terrapins they had seen while on a school outing to our Information Centre.

It was encouraging to know that there were still breeding adults of this terrapin species surviving in the wild in what we considered a less than optimal habitat. The adult yellow-bellied terrapins in our captive breeding project were proving difficult to breed, despite their being strong and healthy. When they did lay eggs we had difficulty with the correct combination of temperature and humidity in the incubators. Another problem was understanding the mating behaviour of what is in essence a nomadic species. Keeping an equal number of both sexes in one large pond had not produced the results we had seen from the smaller black mud terrapins under the same conditions. The arrangement in our new more secure enclosure consisted of four slightly smaller ponds and eight shallow ponds for the juveniles, where we could also isolate individuals to observe their behaviour.

Roger carried his precious cargo to the laboratory where we prepared an aquarium with clean, fresh water and some flat pieces of rock on which the terrapin could rest or bask. I explained to the Dubignon boys that we needed to keep the terrapin in quarantine for a while before he could join the inquisitive gang of black mud terrapins in the large glass aquarium.

The successful breeding of the black mud terrapins put us on notice that we needed to have a detailed assessment of the suitability of the marsh at Grande Barbe on the other side of the island. The extensive marsh, the wide coastal plateau and the fact that only half a dozen people lived there also made it a possible release site for the tortoises when their numbers increased. A survey of the vegetation and habitat quality was needed before we committed any of the terrapins or tortoises to Grande Barbe. In April 2001 Dave Simpson and Audrey Royo dedicated their time as volunteers to mapping the vegetation of the area around the marsh and assessing its suitability for both tortoises and terrapins.

Over the next few months while we concentrated on the animals, our lowland forest trail and the visitors, the volunteers were asked to help with work in the forest area around Jardin Marron. We had decided that until we could solve the problem of getting a larger and more permanent workforce, our best option was to concentrate on several core area in the forest where we could protect and cultivate endemic and native plants.

The work involved sending our pairs of volunteers on a daily hike up into the mountains followed by three or four hours of weeding out the remains of a plot of Patchouli. This aromatic plant, like the coffee plantation, had been established as a commercial venture and then abandoned, leaving the self-seeding plants to thrive on the forest floor. Weeding was not what Aurelie, a French volunteer, anticipated. She made her feelings known and her early departure made it difficult for us to send Nadine Clark into the forest on her own each day. We found her something far less physical to do for the last two weeks of her stay. We asked her if she would prefer to spend time in the quiet, cool, solitude of the sheath-tailed bat roost, to observe and monitor the day-time activity and vocalisation of these small insectivorous bats.

The roost under the jumble of huge granite boulders on the steep hillside was only about one hundred metres from the Information Centre. There were two parts to the roost in this maze of rocks, the first part that I had visited some years earlier was quite easily entered. The other necessitated a very awkward crawl through

a low ceilinged dog-leg passage. When we first started monitoring the bats there were about ten, possibly even fifteen, bats sharing the two roosting areas. Historically, sheath-tailed bats had been reported to be a fairly common species but for no apparent reason had suffered a catastrophic decline to the point where they were now considered to be critically endangered.

The vegetation surrounding the boulder field was a mixture of endemic palms and shrubs heavily invaded by coconuts, cinnamon and a rampant creeper smothering all that was in its path. Justin had already devoted considerable time to the removal of the creeper around the roost and after the interesting and valuable data gathered by Nadine we decided to clear some of the cinnamon away from the entrance to the lower roost. This was of necessity a slow and quiet pruning task so as not to disturb the bats.

In August and September we had two young English volunteers, Mark and Zöe who were asked to continue the work that Aurelie and Nadine had been doing at Jardin Marron. They worked well for a while until Zöe fell ill and it was decided that she should return home, leaving Mark to complete their part of the project. Zöe was the first person we met who had an international roaming mobile telephone that allowed her to speak to her mother in England. We couldn't understand why someone thousands of miles away from home on a remote tropical island could not enjoy the experience of solitude and a disconnect from busy civilisation. How were we to know that these mobile phones were just another invasive species that would creep into the handbags and pockets of almost every human being on the planet, destroying conversations, attention spans and the peace and quiet of the people nearby.

Later in the year we had help at Jardin Marron from a totally unexpected source. A group of staff from the coastguards came to Silhouette for a weekend and offered to help us with our conservation projects. We asked them to uproot all the invasive *Clidemia hirta* shrubs that prospered so well in the sunlit patches along the trail and in Jardin Marron.

They were also asked to ring-bark several enormous Albizzia trees that were spreading in the forest. These were extremely fast growing soft-wood trees that had been introduced onto the islands and were a dominating visible presence as they towered above the natural forest. Ring-barking would kill the trees and avoid the extensive damage that would result from felling them.

We saw ring-barking as the best option because the trees would slowly

disintegrate, losing first the leaves, then the branches and the thicker limbs, leaving only the thick trunk standing. This gave us time to weed out any Albizzia saplings and allow any plants that had been crowded out by the invasive species to establish themselves. Eventually when the termites felled what remained of the trunk the damage to the regenerating forest would be minimal.

Up on the slopes of Mont Poules Marrons, above the bat roost, there were one or two large Albizzia trees. One was depressingly healthy but the other looked as though the termites had taken matters into their own hands. It had some foliage at the base of the trunk but higher up the bleached skeletal limbs were fit only as a look-out post for kestrels.

On the lower slopes, at about the same altitude as the bat roost, in the slowly improving habitat in and around the lowland forest trail, we recorded more frequent visits by the feeding bats. Here we found only two Albizzia saplings to deal with. The gradual regeneration of the natural vegetation and its benefit to the bats was the incentive that drew us away from the tortoises and the visitors on many afternoons. Wandering around in the forest and a bit of gardening were a pleasure just so long as it took place before the mosquitoes got out their blood transfusion equipment.

CHAPTER SEVEN

The gentle whisper of the monsoon rain sweeping across the forest canopy slowly became a murmur as it approached, then a momentary pause as it swept across a grassy field before turning into a thundering roar drumming down on the corrugated iron roof. An endless deluge throughout the night continued into the morning and all day long. Shrugged off by the weather-beaten granite mountain towering above us and the forest that clung to it, the rainwater found a myriad of small channels that fed into the gushing drainage ditch along the foot of the mountain and into the rain-pitted marsh.

On the far side of the marsh is a sometimes ephemeral stream, bordered on one side by the lowland forest trail area and on the other side by precipitous banks which rise to an equally steep short section of built-up road. The monsoon rain came in a turbulent torrent down the tortuous rock-strewn stream bed, flooding the cultivated yam field on the marsh shore.

As the rain continued to fall, the marsh gradually spread out of its usual confines, flooding across the muddy banks into the fields of beach morning glory and mangrove ferns. The sea had built a protective barrier of sand across the marsh exit during the dry season which would hold the flooding marsh in place temporarily until the forest debris settled. On the next ebb tide, the flooded marsh would breach the sand barrier and discharge its unpolluted fresh water onto the tidal flats, to be absorbed by the sea.

On those rain-drenched days we could have stayed in bed, but there were always things to be done. There were specimens to sort out, more seashells to identify and sometimes twenty or more pages of yet another government preparatory draft document for the GEF project to read through and comment on. The more pressing issue though was to try making sense of what was wrong with the wretched computer and it insistence that we had "performed an illegal act"! I phoned Sam Gardner, our computer problem solver, who said something about insects that I did not catch because of the drumming rain on the roof. The more we tried, the less we understood. Frustrated, I phoned Sam again and he agreed to have a look at the computer if we could get it to Mahé. Bugs, he said, not insects!

In the real world, if it ever stopped raining, insects were far more appealing than Sam's bugs. The bee hawk months and the extremely rare humming bird hawk-moths were always a pleasure to watch. We often saw them in the late afternoon, feeding on the flowers of the *Lantana camara* bush that grew out of the retaining wall the Daubans had built to create the level ground in front of the mausoleum. The avenue of bluish-coloured Mauritian palms that line the path from the road to the mausoleum were no longer all present, some having decayed with old age.

It had taken some persuasion on our part to get agreement from the owner to make a new tortoise enclosure on the flat ground in front of the mausoleum. His Aldabra tortoises, once crowded into a nasty little pen at the back of Jimmy's house, were now the occupants of this spacious shady enclosure. The absent sun and the pouring rain only served to encourage the tortoises to retreat into the security of their shells and sleep until the warmth of the sun on another day gave them the energy to get up and wander about.

On the seaward side of the marsh our tortoise enclosures had been extended at the time of the construction of the Information Centre. We now had a third enclosure which gave us the extra space in which to isolate the females when they showed signs of wanting to dig nests and lay eggs. Four years of torch-lit watching, of the lengthy preparations; digging, laying and covering the nests had meant evenings of late dinners, getting soaked on rainy nights and then watching the eggs in the incubators exceed their anticipated hatch-by date. There was no explanation of why the eggs were not fertile; the females were healthy, the eggs looked good but obviously lacked that little ingredient that put life into eggs. A male problem then? All we could do was to treat the tortoises gently, care for them and give them the best food we could find. Given time, tortoise time, we were sure they would find that little spark of life.

The tortoises were an important element in our plans to restore the natural environment to those areas of Silhouette where it would be practical to do so. As the only herbivore that had been part of the ecosystem before the arrival of humans on these granite islands, they played an essential role in maintaining the quality of the vegetation. There were areas we considered suitable for both restoration and as reasonable tortoise habitat, but without exception would need a serious investment of time and labour. The least demanding sites, and therefore our obvious first choices, were the plateau at Grande Barbe and an abandoned piece of farmland on the mountainside at Belle Vue on the way to Anse Mondon.

Beyond consideration were those coastal areas that Justin and I had explored with a view to their suitability. We had made a somewhat hazardous visit to the area above Pointe Civine, the so-called southern reserve. It had some superb vegetation; a mix of species that could survive the months of dry south easterly trade-winds blowing over the slabs of rock. The main problem for tortoises was that the predominant landscape feature was bare granite that held no permanent water.

A more promising, less harsh option would have been the relatively flat area beyond Grande Barbe at Pointe Etienne where there was an abandoned coconut plantation. The amount of work that was needed was however beyond the capabilities of our limited purely voluntary conservation organisation.

Some help for less demanding projects came in the form of a collaboration with Sussex University. The annual field course for the geography students was to take place on Silhouette with the students having access to the facilities and collections in our laboratory. The course was run by Dominic Kniverton and Mick Frogley and included a laboratory technician, Steve Barnes, and later Tim Cane. Justin accompanied the Sussex group, showing the students the elements of plant and animal monitoring in areas of Silhouette where we would benefit from further data gathering. The students were also given the opportunity to involve themselves in hands-on conservation work. They were, for instance, present when the first black mud terrapins were fitted with tiny radio tags as part of our reintroduction programme. They accompanied Justin and Jules on the long hike over the mountain to Grande Barbe and helped release the terrapins into the marsh.

The Sussex students and their supervisors were, like our earlier volunteers, accommodated in the company guest house. The limited space and resultant overcrowding persuaded us that a permanent volunteer building would be less expensive for the students and easier for the field course organisers. We had been corresponding with one of our important sponsors on exactly this same subject. The Swiss organisation, SAN, run by the generous Peter Kistler, had offered to sponsor volunteers who would, in the first instance, build the volunteer centre for future volunteers to assist with our conservation work.

The closest derelict building to our Information Centre was the long narrow wooden building on the hillside adjacent to the Grande Case. We understood this building to have been the nurse's house situated behind the hospital, dating back to the days of Catherine Dauban. Justin, Mick, Dom and I climbed the concrete steps to the house to see if it would serve as a dormitory. We thought it a distinct possibility with enough space at one end to build a small kitchen. Toilets and showers already existed in the out-building at the Grande Case.

When I presented this idea and the proffered funding to the owner it was turned down because he had other plans for the building. Whatever these plans were, they certainly came to nought as a few months later the building was demolished and all that remains are the steps and a concrete foundation; a sad reminder of an historically important building.

(Photo: Guy van Heygen)

Although he was otherwise employed, Jules was finding more and more excuses to spend time helping us. He had become an important member of our small team. A bright young man, he soon learned the botanical names for all the plants and with this knowledge and his pleasant manner he became an excellent guide. Gill and I handled the 1,064 day visitors who came to Silhouette in 2002, while Jules helped by taking some of the hotel guests on the hike to Jardin Marron that year. We were pleased too when the new headmaster at the primary school, who was a bit stand-offish with me, asked Jules to continue the talks to the children. When we first set up on Silhouette, giving the occasional talk and slide show at the school had been at the suggestion of the very pleasant headmistress, so we were pleased that Jules had been asked to continue talking to the children about the island's natural history.

There were however, two unfortunate incidents that involved some of these same primary school children. In August 2002 one of the workers and his two sons arrived at the Information Centre carrying a Seychelles kestrel that one of the lads had shot with a catapult. The father was very apologetic and the boys had obviously been chastised. These beautiful diminutive kestrels are the only raptors on Silhouette, seen quite frequently in the coastal areas and in the village. There was a nest in the old cold store building which was probably the roosting place for this bird with its dangling broken wing.

The break was close to its shoulder where I managed to tape a splint and strap the wing against its body so that it was immobile. The veterinary department on Mahé suggested I give the kestrel a course of antibiotics which the clinic kindly donated. Some weeks later, two German vets who were staying at the Lodge checked the wing for me and said it had mended. Without the restrictive binding the kestrel was able to exercise the wing in the confines of the cage. A week later, I tried to release the kestrel but it floundered and fluttered across the tortoise enclosure

unable to get airborne. A few days later its appetite had returned with a vengeance and the remains of the second of two rats needed removing from the cage. I lifted the lid only high enough to get my arm through and in that instant the kestrel slipped through the gap. It flew across the enclosure, then made a fluttering circuit of the marsh, settling on a fence-post, gave a good shudder to rearrange its feathers before starting to preen itself and enjoy freedom once more.

The second incident was far more disturbing than the happy ending for the kestrel. The nurse from the clinic and her two very upset children arrived carrying a beautiful white-tailed tropic bird with its mascara-like eye-liner and long straight tail feathers. Its glossy white feathers were covered in blood and both its wings broken.

"What kind of children did this?" the nurse asked, tears in her eyes.

"Why have they hurt it?" asked our grandson, Oliver, also on the verge of tears.

"Why indeed ?!" Unlike the tough little kestrel, the tropic bird did not survive the next twelve hours.

For many years I had been writing a weekly natural history column for one of the local newspapers "Regar", as it was known was opposed to the government but my articles were about the fauna and flora, not about politics. I wrote a short piece, asking that question "Why?" When we had tried to involve the children in the conservation of nature why did they still feel the need for cruelty and especially cruelty to such beautiful birds?

It was, I thought, a universal question, not particularly aimed at the children on Silhouette. This was not the way the owner saw it; he saw it as a criticism of the inhabitants of his island and a political criticism as it had been published in the opposition press. I was issued with an ultimatum:

"Stop writing for 'Regar' or pack up and leave Silhouette."

"Oh, sorry Daddy, I won't do it again", crossed my mind: childhood memories of angry words and punishment.

Hurt feelings and a minor fracture in relations with the owner aside, there was no choice to make. We were in no position to abandon our commitment to conservation on Silhouette, nor to walk away from the investments made by our many generous supporters. We stayed put and I apologised to the editor of "Regar" for my sudden silence. Besides, we had other things on our minds at the time. After five years of infertility, the tortoises had finally found the secret of putting life into their eggs. We had two hatchlings from our youngest female, Josephine and then three more from Betty, our smallest and probably middle-aged female. Suddenly we were faced with a whole new set of tortoise needs to learn about.

CHAPTER EIGHT

As the monsoon rains of 2003 came to an end and the islands slumped into the torpid calm of the doldrums, the female tortoises began to show an interest in digging holes and laying eggs.

Between the months of December and April, the male tortoises had been in hot pursuit of the most accommodating females, but now as the north-westerly winds died away the female tortoises withdrew their favours. It wasn't until the beautiful clear, calm, humid days were swept away by the first fresh breath of the south-east trade winds that their minds turned to the serious business of nesting. Two more eggs from Josephine hatched in 2002 but were totally eclipsed by the forty hatchlings that emerged from five clutches laid by Alida. We were at last being rewarded for our patience and for collecting several tons of food for them, to say nothing of the bags of tortoise manure that had gone into the village vegetable patches.

It occurred to us that the baby tortoises were probably a valuable asset that could fund not only the tortoise conservation project, but could also support other research projects that were difficult to finance. The plan was that visitors to the project would be offered the opportunity to adopt a baby tortoise, give it a name and in return, receive an adoption certificate and regular updates on the project by way of our tortoise newsletter.

This worked particularly well in the season when expedition cruise ships came into Seychelles waters as they all included a call to Silhouette and a visit to the tortoise project. "Caledonian Star" was the first and most serious natural history cruise, followed by the large French yacht, "Le Ponant", and our favourite small ship, "Hebridean Spirit". The staff were, without exception, very supportive and some of the passengers became generous sponsors of our tortoise adoption scheme, adopting one, or occasionally, two tortoises. The exception was to have eight hatchlings adopted by one couple for each of their grandchildren. Judy and Stephen Cockburn were among the first to respond to our scheme and also returned to Silhouette to see the tortoises when Justin organised a special trip that included Jan Louwmann, a member of the Nederlands-Belgische Schilpadden Vereeniging and the owner of the Wassenaar Zoo.

When Justin returned a few weeks later with the Sussex University field course, he had three projects to involve them in; terrapins, bats and the mapping of the distribution of endangered plants. Six of our captive-bred black mud terrapins were taken over the island to Grande Barbe for release into the marsh where the adults had been released the previous year.

Two members of the student group were directed to the sheath-tailed bat roost where they were to study the behaviour of the bats in the roost. It was their observations and photographs that led us to believe that our improvements to the health of the natural forest near the roost was the likely reason for the increase in the number of bats using the roost.

On the day preceding the hike to map the plants in the Anse Mondon valley, the students spent the morning collecting all the plastic flotsam and jetsam that had washed up along the beaches of Anse Lascars and Anse Patates – an amazing pile of rubbish thrown overboard into the world's biggest dustbin, the sea.

The hike to Anse Mondon was a long slow climb from La Passe past the abandoned farm at Belle Vue and then down a very steep winding path to the bottom of the valley and yet another recently abandoned house and banana plantation. To reach the plants it was necessary to take the left-hand branch on the permanent stream that made its way down the steep valley.

Halfway up the stream-bed, several very old trees clung to the rock-strewn banks, their roots gripping the huge boulders like gigantic arthritic hands, their trunks warped, twisted, sometimes hollow; veritable fairytale trees. And beyond, growing between the rocks and even thriving in leaf-litter filled pockets on top of the boulders, *Impatiens gordonii* – Busy Lizzie! It might seem strange that such a common plant would need protection, but this particular species is endemic to Seychelles and had all but disappeared from the high forest on Mahé, but here in the Anse Mondon valley scores of plants thrived in an undisturbed isolated stream-bed. The students were set to mapping the extent of this patch where the *Impatiens* grew and to collect cuttings that we could use to establish a second population at Jardin Marron.

The *Impatiens* were also of interest to a botanist from the Eden Project, Alistair Griffiths. He had collected samples and seeds from the single remaining plant that survived on Morne Seychellois on Mahé and came to Silhouette to look at the habitat and collect more seeds. Some months later one of our scientific visitors, Christine Oliver, spent time investigating the likely pollinators of *Impatiens* plants but the weather was not kind to her; heavy rain frightening away the pollinators and drenching her to the skin every time she tried to spend a night waiting for the pollinators.

There were several other scientific investigators on the island that year. The first was a French botanist, Germinal Rouan, collecting and identifying ferns. Then there was an Austrian invertebrate specialist, Michael Madl, who came to the island with our Trust members, Pat and Mo, to collect wasps. Shortly afterwards, we were visited by a really charming French biologist, Daniel Lachaise, with a special interest in the tiny drosophila fruit flies, followed by Massimo Pandolfi, an Italian ornithologist, to set up a project for his students to study the kestrel population on Silhouette. It was gratifying for us to have the laboratory and Information Centre performing its intended function. There was a benefit for the owner as well, with the influx of full-board guests in the guesthouse.

A French biologist, Renaud Boistel, came to study the small leaf litter-inhabiting frogs. He was particularly interested in the largest frogs, about 50 mm. long, known as Thomasset's frog, named for an early plantation owner, and seen most often on the rocks near to permanent water and sometimes on plants. Nothing was known about their behaviour or breeding. Renaud caught some of these frogs and the smaller sooglossid frogs to take back to France for his research project. They were kept in the vivaria in the air-conditioned Information Centre for the duration of his stay. By chance he had also found some Thomasset's frog eggs which we watched develop slowly into tadpoles. Whether the tadpoles need parental care like the sooglossid frogs or simply find their way into the water remains a mystery.

Guy, who was more interested in chameleons and green Phelsuma day geckos than frogs, had been out with his son, Emmanuel, as volunteers when we were away in June. He returned again towards the end of the year when Gill and I were invited as Chair and Secretary of the Nature Protection Trust to attend the World Parks Conference in South Africa, where Nelson Mandela was the guest of honour at the opening ceremony. During the conference we chatted with our compatriots from Conservation and National Parks about the future of Silhouette. The island, or more precisely, the sea around it, had been declared a

Marine National Park back in 1987 but in reality the only protection came from Mahé when we, or the Silhouette island manager, reported seeing boats fishing for lobsters or sea cucumbers.

We had, of course, tried to raise the subject of protection for areas of Silhouette in 1999 when in discussions with the Global Environment Facility consultant and the Department of Forestry but, as mentioned before, that proposal had been metamorphosed by government into the bureaucratic country-wide Mainstreaming Biodiversity Programme. News of our proposal had, however, come to the notice of a Monsieur Batisse at UNESCO who suggested that he would support an application from us to create a Biosphere Reserve that would include Silhouette, North Island and Aride Island, plus the marine area between these islands. M. Batisse was totally flummoxed, even hurt, when explained that the owner had turned us down, saying that reserve status would pose restrictions on his management and development plans for the island. Besides which, an internationally registered biosphere reserve would require financial input where no finance was available, a statement M. Batisse could not understand.

During our absence at the conference, Guy and Jules had looked after things for us. A month later when "Hebridean Spirit" returned, we were offered our, by then usual, five star working holiday on board. Ann and Bill volunteered to stay in the house and deal with the visitors while Jules fed and cleaned the tortoises. We had been back almost three months preparing for the start of the tortoise nesting season when Justin arrived with Mick and Dom and the Sussex University students for the 2004 field course which had attracted enough participants to run two consecutive courses. Kristine Grayson and her partner, John, arrived at the same time and were to spend most of their time at Grande Barbe adding to the earlier vegetation study that Dave and Audrey had undertaken.

Grande Barbe was known to us as the best sea turtle nesting beach on the island but was difficult for us to monitor in any meaningful way. We had tried to interest the residents of the tiny settlement there to count turtles, even offered to pay them to do so. They only ever produced one month's data, for December 2001, when they recorded 22 turtles struggling up the beach and into the beach-crest vegetation where 16 nests were excavated and eggs laid.

An opportunity to collect some consistent and accurate data came about when our website was noticed by Global Vision International, an organisation that offered to bring conservation volunteers for projects like ours. Their representative, Steve Guenin, came to Silhouette to look at the available accommodation – our perpetual unsolvable problem. His suggestion was to use the now disused calorifer building which, I thought, was not unlike the Black Hole of Calcutta with its lack of any windows and smoke blackened walls.

"Maybe, just maybe", he thought, "something could be done about putting some windows in and strengthening the drying racks for use as bunks."

Fortunately, just before I was talked into something so ridiculous, we bumped into Justin Moustache on a visit to the island.

"You can't be serious!" was his shocked comment.

When we explained that the GVI volunteers would be spending most of their time at Grande Barbe, he had a better solution.

"Not all of the A-frame houses are occupied." he said.

"Let's see if I can get permission for you to use one as a base."

Helen and John, the coordinators of GVI came over a few weeks later and we went to inspect the house at Grande Barbe. It was really only one large room with a kitchen and bathroom. The volunteers were to bring their own bedding and supplies, while we had to find a gas cooker and a small fridge. We agreed that the hike over the mountain on the day of arrival and the departure day would be part of the adventure of living for a short while on a remote island. The first volunteers were to arrive in November at the start of the hawksbill turtle nesting season. On our side of the island, from Anse Patates to the far end of Baie Cipailles, we recorded turtle nests in an opportunistic way, relying on the visitors at the Lodge to tell us when and where they saw turtle tracks on their walks along the beaches.

There was nothing opportunistic about recording tortoise nesting activity. We kept a close watch on both mating and egg-laying and were rewarded that year with a further 45 hatchlings from Alida and 10 from Josephine, bringing the total number of baby tortoises to almost 100. This success brought with it pressure to build a large juvenile tortoise enclosure. Being small and vulnerable to rats, cats and prying human hands made their security a priority. With help from Jules, we built a large A-framed enclosure. It was three metres wide by ten long and covered in strong wire mesh, had a shallow concrete wallow and was planted with grass and shrubs in preparation for the largest of the juveniles.

In the midst of all this activity we sensed that something was afoot at the Lodge. Ornella, usually very friendly and chatty, seemed unusually withdrawn and reticent. It wasn't until, returning to Silhouette on the boat one day, I met Harry Tirant, an architect friend from Mahé, who told me that the Lodge was being sold and a new hotel would be built in its place. It appeared that the plan was to use

the Grande Case as the hotel reception area for the new hotel which was going to be of a high standard and very environmentally friendly – whatever that meant. As mentioned earlier, the Grande Case was, as far as we knew, still leased to the Fernier group, as we called the French consortium that had bought the island in 1971.

We had enjoyed the company of Jean-Jacques Fernier and his associates and had the pleasure of dining with them at the Lodge. We had, however, never met Monsieur Bideau who appeared to be their new representative on Silhouette. A rather large, jovial man whose French was a little difficult to understand. M. Bideau explained that in return for foregoing the lease on the Grande case, they had been offered a new lease on the land between the tortoise enclosures and the beach. As a compensation for crowding us out, he offered to build us a new Information centre where the old rusting calorifer stood.

It was such an easy promise for him to make because he was under the impression that the owner would take to heart any suggestions he made. Nevertheless, I spent some time sketching out a few ideas for a new Information Centre that would incorporate an office for our Nature Protection Trust, a laboratory and space to display our ever increasing specimen collection and a display area for fund-raising items and our craftwork. The latter was important because our studio at Beau Vallon had been repossessed by government and then demolished, leaving us with Silhouette as our only outlet.

Dreams aside, the reality was that a major hotel company from the Maldive Islands had bought the lease on the Lodge and all the land once occupied by the poultry farm. The new hotel would replace Ornella's twelve palm thatched bungalows with 112 individual rooms plus all the ancillary buildings required by a hotel of that size.

In a gesture of courtesy, the director of the hotel development, the manager of the Sri Lankan building company contracted to carry out the building, and their assistants, came to assure us that they would incorporate us into the hotel brochures and activities.

"You are talking of two years with no hotel guests", I reminded the director. "We rely on hotel guests for our livelihood and support for our conservation work."

"Well", he said, "I'm not sure what to suggest. As developers we cannot be seen to be paying money to a conservation organisation in case it is seen as a bribe to let us do something we should not be doing in the environment."

We stood in silence for a while, watching the tortoises in the enclosure.

"What about paying me personally to act as your environment consultant?" I suggested.

Our largest tortoise, Adam, was standing at full stretch against the fence, being stroked by one of the group.

"That might work. I will confirm it in the next few days."

As we walked away from the tortoise enclosures he asked if there were any immediate concerns for the environment that they could help with.

My thoughts turned to the insect fogging around the Grande Case some months earlier which we thought would affect the nearby sheath-tailed bat roost. Would a major renovation of the Grande Case have an impact on the bats, I wondered? Protection of the roost had also appeared as a requirement in the EIA for the hotel development.

"There is the roost of critically endangered bats very close to the Grande Case which we would like to monitor in a more permanent way. If we could put a camera in the roost, connected to a monitor in the Information Centre, that would enable us to see if the building work has an impact", I said. We had been told of exactly such a system being used in South Africa to observe hornbills in their nests.

"Get a quote", he said, "and we will fund it."

CHAPTER NINE

The acquisition of the lease by the Maldivian company did not come into force until the beginning of January when we were told that the Lodge would finally close down. We had a really good working relationship with the Lodge and would sorely miss Ornella, Sabrina and Mario, who invited us for a last meal on the evening of Christmas Day. Replete with food and wine, hugs and kisses, we dawdled along the sandy road home, stopping to search the inky blackness of the cloudless night sky for the constellations of Scorpio and the Southern Cross.

At sunrise, over our habitual early morning coffee, we were shocked to hear the news of the devastating earthquake off Indonesia and the subsequent tsunami. Shortly afterwards we had a frantic call from Gill's brother, Steve, in the U.K. worrying about our safety. We never did discover what he was doing listening to the radio so early on Boxing Day morning but decided it best to ask the meteorological department if they considered us to be in any danger.

The man at the other end of the line laughed.

"We are 3,500 kilometres from Indonesia. No, there is no danger."

Still, we fretted about the possibility of an extra large wave sweeping over the beach-crest, flooding the tortoise enclosures, maybe even washing the tortoises out to sea? We could make a dash up onto the brow of the hill between us and Anse Lascars, but what to do about the tortoises…?

As the morning hours passed and we saw the first television images of the destruction and heard the news from Sri Lanka and the Maldives, we began to doubt the reassurance of the weather man. The phone rang. An acquaintance on Mahé told us that Victoria had been flooded and there were rumours of fish swimming in the central police station. He was at Beau Vallon, where he said the sea was behaving strangely.

We did the exact opposite of what we should have done in such circumstances. We dashed down to the beach to see what was happening. At first glance it seemed as though the sea had drained away; the entire reef flat was exposed all the way to the outer reef where the last of the tide was cascading over the coral like a waterfall. Then, quite suddenly, the tide was rising, surging up and up until it almost reached the very top of the beach-crest. And then, it all ebbed away to the edge of the reef again, all in a matter of two minutes. These rapid tides continued all afternoon and into the evening when we felt the worst was over and the tortoises safe.

Mario and Ornella were not one hundred percent convinced of the safety of their hotel guests and, before the next scheduled high tide, decided to move them all to the small church that stood on high ground above the Lodge. In the morning they all trooped back to the comfort of their rooms and a hearty breakfast, one or two weary guests debating whether being safe from the tsunami in the sanctity of the church was worth the centipede bites they now nursed.

That quiet Christmas dinner at the Lodge was a tranquil moment in a year when the once peaceful world around us was in a state of flux. We saw a metaphor for our response to the many changes echoed in the repetitive tides of that 2004 Boxing Day tsunami. At full flow, the sea hissing angrily up the beach, almost overwhelming the beach-crest vegetation, then rapidly ebbing away with a sigh of relief. Emotional upheaval one minute, respite the next.

Some months before the handover there was a sudden increase in the number of Indian builders. They had come to deal with the relocation of those inhabitants living on the land designated as the new hotel property. The disused cold store where a pair of kestrels nested in the roof had to be demolished to make way for the new primary school. On our once tranquil doorstep, corrugated iron stores and an office sprang up, the concrete pad where once copra and cinnamon were sun-dried became a store for building materials and the calorifer became the carpentry workshop. A kitchen with an open wood fire was tucked in at the foot of the mountain, a mere 50 metres from the bat roost.

Not wanting to be excluded from the excitement of making loud building noises, we had our leaking tin roof replaced. As we paid no rent, we were obliged to import the necessary corrugated iron sheeting of the approved colour, using our hard won funds. We were, however, grateful to be relieved of the responsibility of paying our Indian neighbours for their labour.

Once the relocation, demolition and rebuilding were underway, our small island with its dwindling Seychellois population saw the first contingent of 700, rising later to 1000, Sri Lankan and Indian builders for the hotel project. They set about building a vast corrugated building materials store on one arm of the harbour and effectively blocked our somewhat oblique view of North Island. The building company brought in several large trucks, mobile cranes and bulldozers, putting the once lonesome tractor to shame.

As far as we could tell, there were no constraints put on the building staff in their leisure time. They came in large groups, climbed over the enclosure fence, taking photographs sitting on the tortoises and were sometimes upset and angry when asked to leave. They were also at liberty to wander over the island, removing fruit from the Jak-fruit trees in the forest that the residents and fruit bats fed on, and on several occasions cut down immature coco de mer nuts at Jardin Marron.

For the first time in the island's history, graffiti appeared on some of the rocks along the forest trail and we were concerned that the turtle nests on the beach at the hotel site were being raided for eggs.

Any complaints on my part were seen as unnecessary criticism aimed at putting the environment in the way of development, not something you would expect from the environment consultant! In any case, who was there to complain to when we came across some of the island staff breaking up Henri Dauban's old wooden pirogue that had been an historical talking point where it stood on the wide verandah of the Dauban's Grande Case.

This beautiful wooden boat with its direct links to the Dauban family and the history of their island, was now no more than strips of broken wood destined for a fire. Angry and panic stricken, I shouted:

"Stop! What on earth are you doing?"

What they were doing was obvious and it was equally obvious that the pirogue was beyond resurrection.

"We are clearing the Grande Case for renovation."

"But why have you destroyed the pirogue? You could have put it at the

Information Centre. We'd have looked after it."

"The boss told us to break it up and burn it!" They burnt it like some old rubbish; didn't even give the wood to the Indian builders for their cooking fire.

While we often felt overwhelmed by the presence of all these foreign workers, there were times when their willingness to be of assistance to us made us grateful for their presence. Our house roof being one such occasion. The hotel building staff helped us by fabricating three strong heavy metal covers for the outdoor baby tortoise enclosures after we discovered three babies had been "tortoise-napped" by, we suspected, some men who came from Mahé to carry out a survey of the land around us.

With no hotel guests and the ending of regular day visitors, we were pleased to be in demand on the expedition cruises for most of the first three months of 2005. We relied heavily on Jules to look after the animals and deal with the occasional visitor. On our return, we soon adapted to this new changed environment. The twice weekly boat connection and the helicopter service had been stopped. The island now had an almost daily ferry service to Mahé and back on the two hotel boats – "Fat Lady" which carried supplies in her hold and wet passengers on her open deck. "Lady Angelina" whose below deck cabin made for a dry but often sea-sickening passage. Neither of these two vessels was particularly suited to the sometimes tempestuous seas of the south-east trade-winds.

My appointment as environment consultant for the hotel was not the most taxing of commitments. During the initial stage of setting out the buildings on the site, I was asked to identify those trees that were protected and those that could be retained by making slight adjustments to the position of the buildings. We also discussed what should and could be grown in the planned nursery so as to maximise the use of native plants. The horticulturists Buddi and Mr. Bere were a pleasure to work with. We went on several expeditions into the foothills to find plants that could be safely moved to the nursery without causing damage to the forest. We were relieved and gratified when they responded to our suggestion that the beach-crest vegetation be retained not only as a screen for the beach-side rooms, but also to protect the habitat for nesting turtles.

Without the presence of tourists on the beaches between La Passe and Anse Patates, we could only record turtle nesting activity by chance. Even though there were infrequent visits to the beaches we recorded four confirmed nests and another eleven disturbed areas that were probably nests. The regular monitoring by GVI at Grande Barbe, however, had produced surprisingly good results. They had seen fresh tracks on 243 occasions, 61 of these turtles had been seen laying eggs and another 134 were assumed to have nested.

One of the interesting discoveries was that some of these turtles nesting on Silhouette had been tagged after laying on other islands in the archipelago. This rather contradicted the notion that all females returned to nest on the beach from which they had hatched.

Nobody cared much about whether tortoises ever returned to the area where they had hatched. Our tortoises probably had not the slightest idea where they were, let alone where they had hatched. They were trying their best to increase their numbers in our enclosures, so much so that we had to build a second large juvenile tortoise enclosure to accommodate the growing herd.

The only females not fulfilling their roles were Clio and Eve, both of whom might have been too old. Eve in particular had a problem of digging nests, straddling the excavation for half an hour without producing any eggs, and then covering the nest as though she had laid. In the hope of solving this, we asked Bertrand Fiol and Hélène Chardon, two French veterinary graduates, for their opinion. Bertrand and Hélène were looking at the health of tortoises on the islands and spent some weeks with us on Silhouette. Before her empty nest period, Eve had only ever laid twice and on both occasions produced over calcified very thick-shelled eggs that we assumed had been retained in her oviducts for the many years she had spent in overcrowded small pens. She was given several doses of Oxytocin to stimulate her reproductive system but unfortunately to no avail. Poor old

Eve, the only tortoises we knew who could smile, never laid another egg.

In early August the kestrels that used to nest in the roof of the old cold store were flying around the newly finished school that now occupied their territory. Their anxious fluttering around the school and their insistent "ka-ti-ti-ti" calls as they searched for a chink in the armour of this new building prompted us to ask for permission to fit a nest-box into one of the two roof dormers.

Not long after the nest-box was in place we were witness to some strange kestrel behaviour. Both kestrels were in the upper branches of a tall breadfruit tree when suddenly the male launched himself into the air and, calling loudly all the while, flew down to the nest-box, back to the female, back to the nest-box where he landed and went into the box, still calling loudly. As the female remained on her perch high in the tree, he decided to return to her and promptly copulated with her. Their new housing arrangements thus settled, they both flew off to another tree nearby and were still there preening themselves when we needed to move on.

At the end of September the school was due to be officially opened and I was horrified to find a streamer of bunting stretched across the roof directly in front of the nest-box. I asked Jules to remove it. Next morning it was back and the island manager (the second since Jimmy left) was there with his arms folded and in a defiantly aggressive mood.

"This is a special day and you can stop interfering," he snarled. "Important people are coming from Mahé."

The kestrels proved to be far more resilient than I imagined. They produced two chicks despite the days of fluttering flags around their nest-box. Our second resident pair that nested in the eaves of the Grande Case were seen feeding a single chick two months later but unfortunately for them, the house was due to be renovated and the new roof would have no accommodating open eaves in which to nest.

The only kestrels using a natural cliff-side nest that we regularly encountered inhabited the huge granite glacis that sloped down to the edge of the sea on the way to Anse Lascars. When we first arrived on Silhouette these

kestrels took exception to the presence of our two dachshunds trotting through their territory. The dogs either didn't notice or chose to ignore the sudden close quarter feinting attacks as the kestrels came dashing up behind them only inches above the ground and then banked steeply only a dachshund's length from contact.

These diminutive kestrels, barely measuring twenty centimetres in length, have dark grey head markings more akin to falcons than kestrels. The deep chestnut brown wings and back contrast with the pale pinky-brown of the breast and belly. Up on the cliffs above Anse Lascars they were difficult to spot against the pink and grey granite rocks.

The adults were always wary in open areas, but we were fortunate that the young birds often perched on a screw-pine growing in a humus-filled depression in the granite, allowing us to approach within easy range for photography.

Kestrel watching was a more-or-less seasonal activity. Not so the bats and the technology required to observe them. We had eventually taken delivery of the camera and the apparatus that would convert the signal from the camera in the roost via a long partially submerged coaxial cable to the computer monitor in the

Information Centre. On paper it all sounded very simple but it wasn't.

After weeks of fiddling about in contorted positions in the dark of the bat roost, we managed to coordinate the settings on the camera with those at the other end of the cable. It all came to an erratic end when I connected the positive end of the cable to the negative point on the camera. A new camera acquired on a short trip to Singapore finally transmitted a reasonable picture that let us watch the bats' behaviour throughout the day and, with the help of an infra-red lamp, at night too.

This tsunami of technical lunacy had fortunately ebbed away when we were given the opportunity to show the consultant for the government's GEF project and members of the Environment Department, what we were learning about the sheath-tailed bats. We all watched the bats on the monitor for a while, we looked at our invertebrate collection, then sat around discussing the tortoise and terrapin projects and other wider conservation issues. We talked briefly about our aspirations for Silhouette, believing that in the long run we too would benefit from the GEF project.

Instead, over the next two or three years, we were to be inundated with project proposal documents, many of them very lengthy. These were all to do with strengthening the environmental coordination between the various government departments; very little to do with actual hands-on conservation. The documents, sent out by e-mail two or three days before the return deadline, had to be downloaded and printed for careful perusal. We were also obliged to submit an annual financial account of the funds we spent on various relevant projects in order to bolster the government's co-financing commitments towards the GEF project. These were funds raised by us and other NGO organisations for our own work but which appeared in the World Bank documents as money contributed by the Seychelles.

Thinking that our support and our concerns mattered to the Ministry of Environment proved to be an illusion when a month before the rains were due, the island manager, accompanied by a mechanical digger and its crew came trundling along the road. They passed the enclosures, skirted the marsh and headed up the hill towards Anse Lascars. On the brow of the hill, opposite the entrance to our lowland forest trail, they set about digging a deep pit that became a burial site for the uneaten food-waste from the canteen which was feeding 1000 staff members.

This was a flagrant abuse of the environment, posing a serious problem when, during the monsoon, the putrid waste leached into the stream and down into the Dauban Marsh and the sea.

I was told once again that I was not to interfere with the developers and my appeal to the Ministry of Environment was ignored.

My status as the hotel project environment consultant went further downhill in November 2005 when the first few mock-up rooms of the hotel were put on show for visiting tour operators. The well-furnished rooms were spacious with large bathrooms opening onto small enclosed gardens. Each room had a large wooden deck with a view of the sea and the beach-crest vegetation. The problem we pointed out to the developer was the wall lights mounted on either side of the glass doors. These lights lit up the walls facing the sea and at night, when sea turtle nests usually hatched, would disorientate the hatchlings and attract them inland away from the sea.

"Why are you always so negative?" was the response. Anyone would have thought I had criticised the shape of the rooms, the bed linen, the towels or the six foot wide television instead of pointing out the need to change the lampshades. Fortunately, Jeanne Mortimer, the government's turtle consultant, agreed with me and new, slightly less inappropriate shades were put over all the deck lights near the beach.

We were slowly coming to terms with the fact that there were many areas of environmental concern where our opinion was not welcome when a calamity of a different kind struck.

Jules and the island manager had an altercation which resulted in both the manager and Jules and his family being abruptly removed from the island. We struggled at first to cope with the loss of someone upon whom we had relied so heavily, but took heart when the new young manager, Kenneth, suggested we employ the partner of one of the school teachers who would otherwise have had no reason to stay on Silhouette. This arrangement only lasted the trial period because the young man was unreliable and not really interested in what we asked him to do. When he left, Kenneth decided to second Roc, a quiet, very smiley island worker, to help feed and clean the tortoises.

Three months before the hotel was scheduled to open, the great tin shed on the harbour had been demolished and a posh new reception centre and landing stage were in the final stages of completion. A concrete helicopter landing pad had been added and an attempt made to get grass growing on the coral fill. At our suggestion Mr. Bere had planted a hedge of *Scaevola* around the harbour edge to soften the brutal hardness of the granite rock facing. Two rather large, fast ferry boats made an appearance and with them came the first dedicated hotel marketing and reception staff. Hot on their heels came the first prospecting tour operators. The hotel was still full of builders, the bars and restaurants in the early stages of staff training, the spa not yet fully equipped and the dive centre almost ready, but not quite.

This meant that we, or at least, the tortoises and the Information Centre, were the main attraction for the tour operators. The more energetic wanted to be taken on nature walks and hikes and we were suddenly no longer just the two grumpy people living at the end of the road.

Among the early arrivals were Dirk and Daniella, who were part owners of the new purpose-built dive centre. Innocents as we were, on our desert island, in the matters of hard-nosed business, we welcomed them into the Information Centre and told them what we did for the visitors. A matter of weeks later we were dismayed to discover they had called the dive centre the "Eco Center" and were planning to take visitors on organised walks led by the foreign staff who would have only our Silhouette pocket guide to tell them what they were looking at. It took us some time to adjust to what we saw as their treachery; an adjustment that came about when the very warm and friendly Italian divers, Lorenzo and Lisabetta, and an English dive master, Ruth, came to introduce themselves. It took a little longer to get to know Dirk and Daniella and settle our differences.

At the end of October 2006, the first five guests arrived at Labriz Silhouette, as the hotel had been named. They were an Italian couple with a small child, and a Swiss couple. The day after their arrival, the excited Swiss couple came to the Information Centre with the news that they had watched a turtle make her way across the beach at Baie Cipailles and deposit a nest full of eggs in the beach-crest vegetation. They waited until she had slipped back into the surf before rushing over to tell us. We were back in business!

CHAPTER TEN

Turtles were not at the top of our list of priorities on the days when we had to weigh and touch up the identification numbers on the juvenile tortoises. Those five barren years when the tortoises seemed incapable of laying fertile eggs had been followed by a biblical four years of plenty. Four years in which Josephine, Alida and Betty had produced 140 hatchlings which were growing at an amazing rate and putting pressure on us to build yet another juvenile enclosure.

Once each month we rigged up a sunshade between the first two A-framed enclosures and set out a table, the scales, a small pot of white enamel paint, paint-brush, pens and paper. Gill and I, and Justin when he was on the island, weighed all the juvenile tortoises, starting from those that were only a few hundred grams to those weighing in the region of ten kilos. Each tortoise had an identification number, prefixed by the mother's initial, painted on the back scute. These numbers usually needed touching up before the tortoise was returned to its enclosure.

One of the important elements in our government-approved management plan for conservation on Silhouette was the reintroduction of the two forms of granite island giant tortoise, *Aldabrachelys hololissa* (a grazing species), and *Aldabrachelys arnoldi*, (a browsing species) into their natural habitat on Silhouette. In 2006 we had 135 *arnoldi* juveniles and some eggs incubating, but we had only five *hololissa* juveniles. We decided it was time to release the adult *arnoldis* and to concentrate on increasing the number of *hololissas*.

When I requested permission to release the five adult *arnoldis* at Grande Barbe, where Dave and Audrey had surveyed and found suitable habitat, I was directed to a new hotel development company that had acquired a lease on the land. It seemed to us to be a strange place to choose to build a hotel on this isolated part of Silhouette which had only very limited seasonal access by sea. The long, very beautiful, beach was divided from the sea by a broad barrier of beach rock, leaving only a limited direct access to the sea where the fresh water flowing out of the marsh suppressed the growth of coral.

The developers readily agreed to the release of the tortoises on their land with the proviso that they would have to be penned during the construction

phase.

Arrangements were made for the release in December when Justin and a group of tortoise enthusiasts and friends were due to visit Silhouette.

The visitors sailed around to Grande Barbe in the charter yacht "Seashell", while Justin and I travelled in the island's pirogue with the tortoises.

We unloaded them where the pirogue had nudged into the beach, allowing the tortoises to wade ashore as though they had floated across the ocean to this part of the island. Unlike their ancestors, these captive tortoises had never seen a beach before and all made their way with tortoise haste into the beach-crest vegetation.

Once satisfied that the tortoises were settled and that our aim of repopulating the island with its natural herbivore had taken a first step, we returned to La Passe and a celebratory dinner on board "Seashell".

Subsequent visits to Grande Barbe confirmed that all five tortoises were in

good health and surviving their wild existence. There was a big contrast between their new lives in the wild and the unnatural turn of events at the Labriz Hotel.

Lorenzo came by one day in January to say that he had seen guests at the hotel putting baby hawksbill turtles into the hotel's fresh-water lake. This confirmed our concerns about the exterior lighting on the chalets being inappropriate. By the end of the month Lorenzo had rescued 25 baby turtles from the lake and we had released them into the sea, opposite the tortoise enclosure where it was dark. The next few weeks saw the rescue of a further 154 hatchlings found wandering inland at the hotel, attracted by the lights.

We discussed the idea of including in the hotel information folder, a one page leaflet concerning turtle nesting and the hatchlings. The manager said he would consider how he could incorporate it into the folder. We had become accustomed to being regarded as a nuisance by the hotel manager and were hurt, but not surprised, to find our A4 colour leaflet reduced to a mere four lines tacked onto the general hotel information.

The turtle nesting season at Grande Barbe had once again been monitored by GVI volunteers. As their last team packed up camp and hiked over to La Passe, came the news that the hotel developer for Grande Barbe had come to the obvious conclusion that they could not build the hotel by bringing the materials in by sea. What was needed was a road from La Passe with its harbour, to Grande Barbe!

It seemed a fairly vague idea at first, and we could not understand how it was financially viable to build a road several kilometres long across uncharted mountainous terrain in order to build a hotel. We hadn't realised that money flowed like rivers of gold in the investment banks at the time, and everything however unreal was financially possible. This new unreality was brought home to us when I was asked to join a group of various government departmental staff and the developer on a route-seeking hike across the island in preparation for the drawing up of an Environment Impact Assessment.

The group did not actually seek anything, merely followed the one and only centuries-old track across Silhouette on its steep winding way up and up through the forest, across the ridge below Gratte Fesse and then down, down, down to the coastal plateau and the harbour at La Passe. Construction difficulties and the probable destruction of many fragile habitats were to be raised in the EIA, but my immediate concern was that any road, built for whatever reason, would attract investors wanting to own property along the route in what was an almost pristine forest environment. My suggestion that some areas, and especially the higher-altitude forest, should be given formal protection was accepted by the developer and by the owner and came to fruition later in the year when the President, attending an international meeting, declared the government's intention of declaring most of Silhouette to be a national park.

While the threat of the road hung heavily over our heads, something else happened that lifted our spirits. We were introduced to the new manager of Labriz, Vinesh Gupta, and his wife, Bernali, with whom we felt an instant rapport. We were no longer the hotel developers' nightmare, we felt we were part of the hotel family. They were fascinated by the tortoises and all the activities in our information centre and keen to help in whatever way they could.

Vinesh offered us the loan of two; sometimes three, of the gardening staff, once a fortnight, to help with the lowland forest trail project, removing alien plants, weeding and even ring-barking some the larger cinnamon trees. On Environment Day, the entire gardening staff, many of the general hotel staff and all the senior staff, including Vinesh, devoted some of their time to helping extend the area we were trying to clear and replant.

An added bonus for us were occasional invitations to eat at the various restaurants in the hotel and an open invitation to Sunday lunch which we limited ourselves to accepting only once a month.

The euphoria of finally having a good working relationship with the hotel was somewhat overwhelmed when Mr. Baghat's truck began dumping building sand and stone on the land between our house and the beach. A large concrete mixer was trundled into position only metres away from our front door. Construction started on what would be four double-storey buildings and a restaurant.

"La Belle Tortue", as it was named, was sometimes to be a holiday apartment complex for the French group, and sometimes a hotel. It

occupied the entire narrow plot of land between the road and the beach. Permission to build right up to the high tide mark was making allowances for foreigners by bending the rules, as was the proposal to re-route our dusty road to the other side of the tortoise enclosures along the edge of the marsh. Mr. Baghat and his men marked the route with a line of wooden stakes driven into the muddy shore of the marsh where they stood like spectres until they rotted away and the threatened road faded into oblivion.

The incessant daytime noise of men and their clanking, grinding machinery manoeuvring along the road and filling the house with diesel fumes was not a very pleasant experience, nor was the difficulty this noise cause when we were talking to visitors at the tortoise enclosures. It was much worse for Gill who looked after the information centre and the NPTS office while I escaped into the silent forest two, sometimes three times a week, taking guided tours up to the tranquillity of Jardin Marron.

As we slowly came to terms with these stressful developments all around us, our one consolation was that one day the builders would complete their task and leave us in peace. In the meantime we still had the Silhouette Conservation Project to run. As a follow-up to the release of the tortoises at Grande Barbe, John Pemberton, a volunteer, spent a month collecting data on the diet and plant preferences of the tortoises. When John left, Justin and Jim Juvic, a tortoise specialist who brought several tracking devices to attach to the released tortoises, trekked over to Grande Barbe. The Sussex University students returned and for three months we shared our laboratory facilities with the Earthwatch marine study group, and Marie-Louise Carriou, a close friend and colleague of the late Daniel Lachaise, came to continue his work on the drosophila flies.

While we were thus occupied and continuing to care for the tortoises, terrapins, bats and frogs, a request came from the person delegated by the owner to write the Environmental Impact Assessment for the Grande Barbe road. We were asked to take on the task of writing the section dealing with the anticipated impact the road would have on the biodiversity along the route.

The extensive data Justin and other scientific collaborators had gathered over the past 16 years enabled us to put together a detailed and thoughtful assessment, covering 14 pages, of the probable impact on the general biodiversity and those endemic and protected plants along the route. We relied also on a study into the plant communities at various altitudes on Silhouette that had been published some years earlier by Zurich University. It was our conclusion that, even taking into account the mitigation measures we proposed, the road posed a serious problem for the biodiversity that made up this fragile environment.

Even though we had been pressed to support the road at the outset, after the initial draft of the EIA had been scrutinized, I was made aware that I had ventured out onto the quicksand of my relationship with the owner. I was not surprised to be told that I was a complete idiot if I thought anyone would ever take notice of what we had written.

The draft EIA, grudgingly accepted with no thanks for our voluntary hard work, was then formalised and submitted to the relevant government departments for final approval. While this process was underway I was asked to accompany the author of the assessment, a representative from the developers, and some engineers on a walk to familiarise them with the route. A broad yellow plastic band, reminiscent of a police crime scene tape, now ran across and beyond the old unspoilt hiking trail.

We had previously concentrated on the impact the road would have on the biodiversity but this time, looking at it from the point of view of the engineers, it soon became apparent that the impact on the landscape would be catastrophic. The steep mountainside would necessitate the road taking sweeping curves to cope with the incline, involving considerable excavations and huge rock retaining walls. On the ridge below Gratte Fesse the existing hiking trail involved a climb up a sixty degree slope from both directions. Here the road would have to make a series of hairpin bends with yet more retaining walls that would completely destroy a totally unique forest habitat supporting invertebrates recorded nowhere else in Seychelles.

"How will you prevent erosion and the surface washing away in the monsoon?" I asked.

"The entire route will be concrete", the prospective Irish builder told me.

My mind boggled. Four kilometres of concrete! How many tons of material and cement would have to be shipped into the harbour and just imagine the transport cost.

"Have you thought about the impact of diesel fumes in this closed forest environment?"

"Not really a problem. After construction we will be using only electric buggies to transport the guests across the island."

"Seriously? Electric buggies? They won't cope with this steep gradient."

"Also not a problem, we are going to have lay-byes with recharging points."

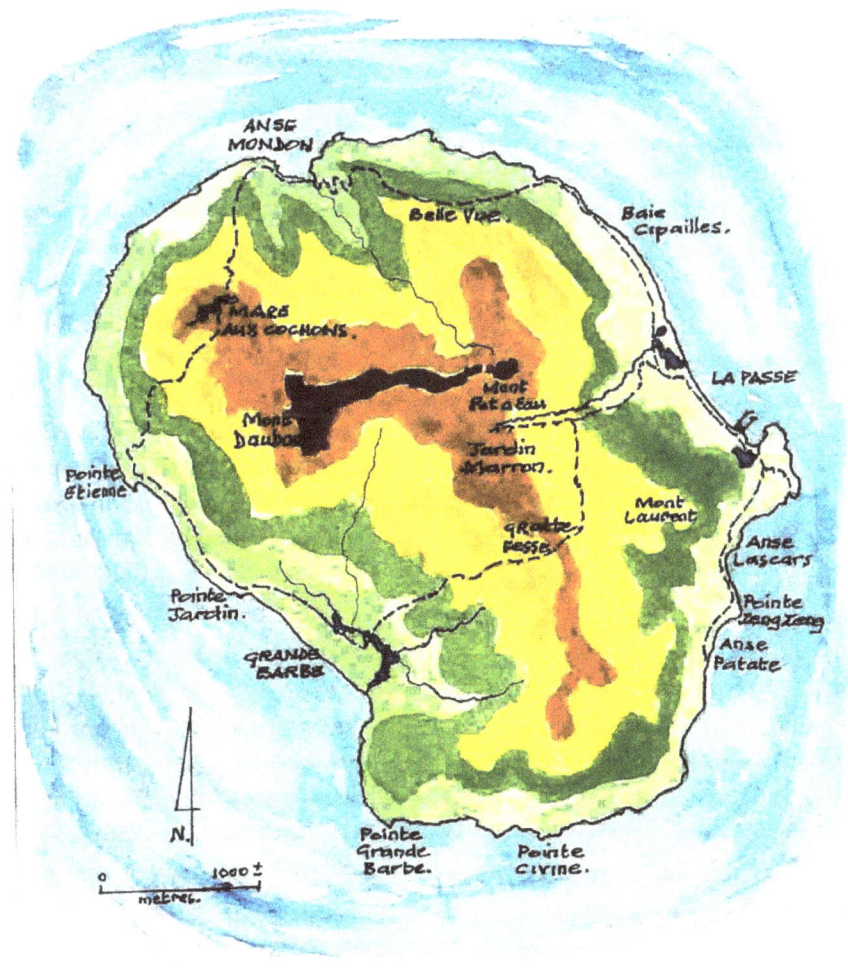

There was no point in pursuing this line of conversation. At Labriz it took several hours to recharge the buggies and I had a vision of the travel-weary hotel guests sitting quietly twiddling their fingers half way up the mountain, waiting while the buggy was recharged.

In the end, none of this mattered because, in its wisdom, the government, contrary to expectations, refused permission for the road project. The developer may have heaved a sigh of relief because the world was soon to learn about Lehmann Brothers, and the banks would see their rivers of gold run dry.

The conservation of nature on Silhouette was, we thought, the reason we were working on the island, but in the eyes of the owner our negative stance on the road project was a betrayal. Initially this forced us into a closer association with the Islands Conservation Society, an organisation closely linked to the owner. I found myself compromised into accepting a place on the board of trustees as the only way to try to understand what their implied intentions were for Silhouette. We made no progress with this approach as they really had no clear idea of what they wanted to do on the island.

Eventually, a "Silhouette Foundation" was imposed upon us by the owner and we were instructed that any new projects should be sanctioned by this Foundation. In theory it was to be an equal partnership but we knew we were outnumbered. There was a vague proposal to build a centre with office space on Silhouette, even though we had no need of another office. Funding for the Foundation would be by way of a conservation levy imposed on the hotel guests, together with a contribution to the running costs paid by the Foundation members. Knowing our own limitations we accepted these new conditions but objected strongly to the demand that we contribute financially to the running of this purely bureaucratic Mahé-based body.

When things became too oppressive, we took ourselves off to the hotel for a quiet coffee or a beer with Vinesh. He would listen to our tales of woe and find some way to lift our spirits. We usually timed these therapeutic meetings for five-thirty when the guests had gone to their rooms to wash and change for dinner, leaving us in the comfortable armchairs enjoying the view across the undisturbed swimming pool. After half an hour of sorting out the world, we wandered back across the wooden walkway that spanned the lake that had once been a damp coastal mudflat. It had become a fresh-water lake, home to large shoals of fish, the occasional moorhen and a lonely old grey heron.

As we three stood on the walkway we told Vinesh of the problems we had had during the previous turtle nesting season – all the hatchlings that had to be rescued because of the room lighting. Vinesh agreed to initiate three measures that we proposed. The first step was to put markers around the nests to prevent guests walking on them. The verandah lights of the rooms nearest the nests would be switched off for a week prior to the anticipated hatching date.

Two large plywood boxes with one narrow side opening would be made, to cover the nests ensuring that hatchlings would be shielded from any hotel lights and the only source of light they would see would be over the sea. With these measure in place we needed to rescue only five hatchlings that season.

The walkway across the lake made landfall a few metres from the hotel reception. Sometimes we hitched a lift on one of the electric buggies if they were on their way to collect guests from the harbour. At other times, we dawdled along the road, stopped for a while at the school to see the kestrels or watched the fruit bats squabbling in the breadfruit trees. On the way home we would pass the harbour and the renovated Grande Case where the staff were busy setting tables and preparing the evening's Creole buffet. The road made a sharp twist around the island manager's office, passed the high concrete walls of the massive new diesel storage farm, through the Indian workers' camp and took us home. The tall ghostly unfinished buildings of La Belle Tortue would be fading into obscurity in the rapidly approaching darkness. The tortoises would be tucked away in their favourite corners, sound asleep and safe.

CHAPTER ELEVEN

On the far side of the Dauban marsh an old spreading fig tree cast its shadow over two immense granite boulders that lay half-submerged in the muddy shore of the marsh. In season, its branches were festooned with thousands of tiny ripening figs and scores of squealing, chattering fruit bats. This gourmet feast was so alluring that the bats were often active throughout the daylight hours; their golden furry bodies in sharp contrast to the black of their leathery wings. Some days they could be seen high above the island, circling on the thermal currents like birds of prey, but when there were figs to eat they cruised over the marsh and made quite spectacular landings in the old fig tree.

The fig tree in the tortoise enclosure was still a mere sapling in comparison and of no interest to the bats. When figs were not in season, they preferred the two breadfruit trees next to the terrapin enclosures. No figs and no breadfruit brought the bats into the Indian almond tree that hung over our bedroom. The incessant squawking arguments and assumed erotic screeching were not nearly as disruptive as the bombing raids of falling fruit onto our tin roof.

Fruit bats had long been considered a culinary delicacy in this part of the world and they had been hunted from the earliest days of colonisation. When the possession of firearms by members of the public was made illegal after the 1977 coup d'état, the hunters became trappers. Fortunately, this activity on Silhouette was on a very small scale and, despite

(Photo Julie Gane)

the cruelty, we did not object until, that is, fruit bats appeared on the Creole menu at the Grande Case restaurant. With talk of Silhouette becoming a National Park and the hotel publicity claiming to be environmentally conscious, they did not take much persuading to remove the bats from the menu. The staff were thereafter careful not to confirm the rumour that they could still be had on special request.

It was a relief that no-one had any culinary desires for the tiny sheath-tailed bats in their hideaway not too far from the Grande Case. There had been a fluctuation in the numbers of bats in the roost which meant that there was probably a secondary roost we had not yet found. On the other hand, on the CCTV camera, we often saw smoke drifting through the roost, smoke originating from the cooking fires at the Indian builders' camp just below the roost. The other possibility was of predation by rats, cats and, it was even suggested, by barn owls. The latter was discounted because we had neither seen nor heard barn owls for over two years. We spread fine beach sand across the tunnel between the two roosting areas but never found cat tracks. For twelve months we set bait and traps for rats but probably only succeeded in poisoning a few hermit crabs.

There were still occasional spells of non-cooperation with the bat camera, but for the most part it worked well and allowed us to store twenty-four hours of data that could be viewed at convenient times. Our technological skills were stretched to the limit when, out of the blue, a German couple who were staying at Labriz, presented us with two portable solar panels for use on one of our projects. These panels and a set of wireless transmitters and receivers were intended to upgrade the CCTV camera system, but involved a considerable amount of time to set up and adjust.

At one point in the proceedings, I clambered up the near-vertical face of the jumble of house-sized granite boulders to help Justin set up an antenna for the transmitters and found that we were in one of the most beautiful features in the Silhouette landscape. It was not a panorama, merely a detail in the forested hillside. We were almost encircled by the weather-worn, smooth undulations in the granite, looking like slow, gentle, oceanic swells now silent and still, raised up into the whispering forest canopy, holding in its grasp a small secret garden of ferns and xerophytic shrubs. This natural sculpture brought a warm sensual moment of pleasure akin to the emotion aroused by the music that lives buried deep in the soul.

We, Justin and I, had been to some incredibly beautiful places on Silhouette where I had not had the same emotional reaction. We had hiked to the far side of Mont Corgat where the curving granite faces disappeared all the way down to the sea. On the summit, tropic-bird orchids with their long spurred white flowers thrived, despite the battering south-east trade winds.

We had struggled up the steep humid slope to the pinnacle of Mont Pot-a-Eau, clinging to the trees and climbing over the shrubs. Here, too, were the clusters of fragrant long tubed pink *Glionettia* flowers and often a kestrel objecting to the invasion of its territory.

We only once took the hazardous climb from Mon Plaisir along La Chaine Catherine towards Mont Dauban, the highest peak on the island. In this cloud forest, the trees were shrouded in thick bands of moss upon which the humidity glittered like gemstones. In places the ridge was only a metre wide with steep cliff faces descending into the forest far below. White-tailed tropic-birds cruised by on the up-draught, their clacking calls echoing off the cliffs. This was Silhouette in all its beauty.

Justin and a Belgian botanist, Bruno Santerre, made other more demanding expeditions into some of the far less accessible places; expeditions beyond my physical capabilities. Bruno was studying plant habitats and building an extensive herbarium collection. The dehumidifier and a large pile of old newspapers in our Information Centre became Bruno's plant laboratory where he sorted and dried his plant specimens.

There was room in the Information Centre for Sara Rocha and her two herpetologist colleagues from Porto University in Portugal to deal with the skinks and geckos they were studying. A chance too to compare them with and collect DNA samples from those in our collection. No sooner had Sara and her team left than we had the pleasure of showing two members of the Madagascar branch of Conservation International around our various projects. The head of CI who came to Silhouette in 2006 had indicated that their interests in Madagascar could have some relevance to our projects. These two visitors were particularly interested in the proposed National Park and the sheath-tailed bat project.

A month later Justin returned from Cambridge with the Sussex University students and their supervisors. They continued their monitoring in areas they had set up the previous year, hiked across to Grande Barbe to check up on the released tortoises, helped in the lowland forest trail and spent a day collecting the rubbish along the shoreline from Anse Patates to Anse Lascars.

Other research projects were running into difficulties though. The annual Earthwatch marine programme was refused permission to return to Silhouette because, it was said, they had not submitted a report on their previous year's research. Our other important turtle monitoring partners, GVI, had a new coordinator who had difficulty organising the boat transfers and objected to the volunteers having to hike through the forest to Grande Barbe. None of this had been a problem when Helen and John were organising the volunteers, but now it was "too dangerous" and GVI withdrew from Silhouette.

We were fortunate to still have the "volunteer" gardeners from the hotel and, once again, the large team of staff to help on Environment Day. Serious gardening, using all the machinery that Mr. Baghat possessed was also underway at La Belle Tortue. Construction of the buildings had been completed, they had been painted, decorated and even furnished. Landscaping, if it could be described as such, took the form of covering the perfectly fertile sandy soil with a thick layer of red earth. The red earth was excavated from a new area in the forest opposite the lowland forest trail with, once again, no thought given to the run-off of red mud making its way into the stream, down to the marsh and out onto the coral reef. To make matters worse, the quarry became a dumping ground for garden waste and not infrequently for plastic bags and general hotel garbage.

The slowly evolving lowland forest trail and the red earth quarry were shown to staff of the Ministry of Environment and Natural Resources when they came to Silhouette to discuss with us, the NGO responsible for conservation on Silhouette, the proposed National Park. We shared a common vision of the design of modern protected areas which we and the government delegation had learned at the IUCN World Parks Congress in Durban in 2003.

Our suggestion to the Ministry was to manage Silhouette as a Category V protected area in much the same way as several parks were managed in France. This would mean the protection of the entire island, its biodiversity and the historical human impact. It would also involve the developed area and those set aside for development, like Grande Barbe, in protecting and caring for the environment.

The IUCN guidelines for setting up new protected areas required that there should be a consultation with all the "stakeholders" involved in the park. This included not only the owner of the land and those with commercial interests like the hotel, but also all the people who lived within and adjacent to the protected area. Assuming that this was a purely National Parks Department process, I offered to produce a questionnaire seeking the opinion of all these "stakeholders". The workers were pleased to be asked and were for the most part very positive with only two people worried about restrictions on collecting medicinal plants. The hotel was nervous about responding in case they committed themselves to something unforeseen. The owner took exception to the damned cheek I had in even asking his workers for their opinion. I should have known from my earlier misdemeanours that the feudal system under which we lived on the island meant that even at the request of government, I had no right to involve myself with anything to do with the future of Silhouette.

The final decision by government was to have a standard National Park system with the Park managed from Mahé, and a basic skeleton staff on the island. All this offered was yet another "paper park" that looked good internationally but did not address the environmental issues that needed a large work-force and sufficient finance.

When the draft EIA for the National Park was circulated we were pleased to see that the boundaries did in fact include most of the island, excluding only the coastal plateau areas at La Passe and Grande Barbe. The area from Pointe Varreur to Anse Patates had also been excluded as a possible development area. This anomaly included the old cemetery and a very rocky stretch of forest parallel to the lowland forest trail. This area we saw as an important feeding area for the sheath-tailed bats and with support from the Species Survival Commission of IUCN, Professor Paul Racey, the IUCN bat specialist, and Conservation International, we managed to have this area included in the National Park.

In an attempt to improve our shaky relationship with the owner, we were trying our best to cooperate with ICS. As members of IUCN we and the government were asked to support the application of ICS to become members of the Union. We also willingly agreed to assist with their project to reintroduce black mud terrapins to North Island. We looked after their fifteen terrapins in quarantine in our enclosure for three months, caring for them and feeding them in preparation for their transfer to North.

At an autocratic ICS meeting I was instructed to submit an annual work-plan for their approval and, over and above our quarterly reports, to submit a detailed annual report on our activities. With the restrictions on any new activities imposed upon us in the guise of the Silhouette Foundation, we devoted our time to the tortoises, terrapins, bats and frogs.

We were trying to find a way of breeding the sooglossid frogs in captivity without much success. In the wild we continued monitoring them in various localities throughout the year, noting the seasonal changes in these habitats and the impact these changes had on the frogs. Our concerns led us to believe that the danger to these tiny leaf litter-inhabiting frogs lay in the possibility that a warming climate would not only raise the ambient temperature so that it would be too high for the survival of the frogs but would also dessicate the leaf litter, making it less supportive of the insects upon which the frogs fed. Justin put together a project that sought funding to purchase several automatic weather stations that would record temperature, rainfall and both atmospheric and soil humidity.

Unlike the sooglossid frogs, tree frogs were not particularly common on Silhouette and were generally to be found near streams where they could lay their spawn. Very occasionally a tree frog appeared in an unexpected place, taking advantage of the more easily caught moths and bugs around electric lights. A pair of these wanderers ended up in a terrarium in the laboratory and in the the latter half of 2008 produced spawn on the side of the sprouting coconut which provided the greenery in which they lived. The spawn was, as we knew it should be, on the husk but  above the water. When the tadpoles emerged they slithered down into the water where they lived like all normal tadpoles. However, when they shed their tails they abandoned their aquatic lives and climbed up into the vegetation where their stillness and exquisite green colour kept them safe.

Not all frogs in Seychelles were as exotic as the tree frogs and the sooglossids. Along the streams, around marshes and in gardens, the Mascarene frogs fulfilled the role of normal frogs. Their sharp "rivet" calls were the common sounds on damp evenings and early mornings.

(Photo: E Greenbaum)

Towards year's end, when the climate in the distant northern hemisphere stiffened into the first signs of the coming winter, we were distracted from our generally terrestrial occupations by the quiet conversational "prit-prit" calls of a flock of bee-eaters flying in wide sweeping circles above the trees, then banking down towards the marsh. They seemed to be intent on hawking insects over the water, but then, as if by consensus, they began to settle in an isolated mangrove in the marsh. More neighbourly conversation and then sudden silence in the rapidly approaching darkness of nightfall.

These beautiful bright green birds with their chestnut coloured throats and black masks turned out to be blue-cheeked

bee-eaters, rare migratory birds to these remote islands and never previously in such large groups. Reports from neighbouring islands suggested the invasion was widespread. There were, we calculated, about seventy bee-eaters that lingered on for several days catching dragonflies and. much to our delight, hunting the yellow paper-wasps that were, along with centipedes, the nastiest bad-tempered creatures on the islands. The instinct to continue their migration to southern Africa drew our unexpected visitors away in small groups until by mid-January, they were all gone and the yellow wasps came out of hiding.

We had had other less spectacular, but equally interesting visitors. There had been a group of young people belonging to the Wildlife Clubs, groups from the National Institute of Education, the Ministry of Environment and even a group of eighteen conservationists from the Micronesian Challenge organisation. They were given talks about the tortoise project, shown around the displays and collections in the Information Centre and given the opportunity to see the live CCTV pictures of the sheath-tailed bats in their roost.

The only visitor not particularly interested in our projects was a very downcast Jean-Jacques Fernier who had come to inspect "La Belle Tortue" which, he said, looked like a row of French suburban houses! These were definitely not his idea of the "Petite Grande Case" he had been expecting. His visit was followed a few weeks later by the most enthusiastic of all our tortoise adoption supporters. Judy and Stephen Cockburn came to see the growing hatchlings they had adopted for their grandchildren. On this visit they added "Zachary" to their tortoise family.

The only unwanted visitor in 2009, if we discounted the flying cockroaches and rhino beetles that ricocheted from light to light in the sitting room, was a wolf-snake that found its way into the office in the house. Although not harmful, these slender constrictors that survive on a diet of frogs, skinks, geckos and even

chameleons, provoke an instinctive fear in most of us. Spotting a wolf-snake resting under her desk, Gill informed me that she was going nowhere near the office until it was snake-free! Over the years we had lived in Seychelles, I had overcome the fear of snakes instilled into me as a child in Africa where almost every snake is venomous.

Aware of those staring eyes and head raised in warning, I had learned to distract the snake with one hand and grab it just below the head with the other hand; a technique I used when we encountered snakes on guided tours into the forest. For the next two days Gill maintained a cautious approach to the office, waiting at the door in anticipation of further serpentine incursions.

In March of 2009 we had a sudden rush of expedition cruise ships to deal with. The French yacht "Le Ponant" came twice, the "Hebridean Spirit" called for the last time before being sold and the "National Geographic Explorer" called twice. Fortunately, Justin had come from Cambridge ahead of the Sussex University annual field trip and was able to help with the tours.

The automatic weather stations that Justin had ordered arrived and with help from the Sussex students, they were placed in sooglossid frog habitats at Jardin Marron and higher up, at Mon Plaisir. There they would make two-hourly recordings that could be downloaded onto the computer at regular intervals. The two weather stations at sea-level would enable us to compare any changes with the more basic data we had been collecting over the years.

Improving the habitat for the sheath-tailed bats was proceeding well with the help of the hotel gardeners. We had also recently acquired a much improved bat recorder with funds donated by Conservation International. Both cameras in the two roosting areas were behaving themselves, providing us with good quality pictures of bat activity. When a national sheath-tailed bat committee was set up, Justin represented NPTS, attended the first meetings and visited the roosts on Mahé, but like the Bird Forum and the National Parks Committee, of which we were members, after two or three meetings the interest of other participants in these well-meaning ventures slowly seeped away.

Gill and I took a much-needed break in May, leaving the tortoises, terrapins and tourists in the capable hands of Ann and Bill, our regular tortoise-sitting volunteers. They coped well with the endless stream of visitors, even those guests who came after dinner at the Grande Case, expecting to get into the Information Centre. At that hour there wasn't much point in looking for tortoises in the dark as they were all tucked up in their shells, parked against the enclosure fences for security.

Later in the year Vinesh brought a consultant from what we understood to be the international group that had financed the hotel project. We took him up into the lowland forest trail to show him how the hotel had supported our rehabilitation work. That afternoon over drinks at Labriz, he broached the subject of setting up what he called a Science Committee that would ensure the hotel was complying with all the terms of the original EIA. It would comprise a representative from the finance company, the hotel management and ourselves as the on-site conservation body. This was one of the goals of the GEF project; tourism working with conservation and we were pleased that it was happening on Silhouette.

The first meeting of this so-called Science Committee was held in the recently opened Labriz reception centre and mooring at Bel Ombre on Mahé. Vinesh and the consultant were there, as was the director of operations for the Maldivian owners of Labriz and their chief accountant. We discussed ways for the hotel to use dedicated staff to monitor turtle nests on the hotel beach, their help with our foresrt rehabilitation and the need for me to hold regular talks about conservation issues with the reception and senior staff. Although we were merely a willing partner seeking to help the hotel meet its EIA commitments, our presence on something called a "science committee" was seen by the owner as an outrageous attempt to undermine the authority of the Silhouette Foundation and weaken their control of the island. There seemed little point in trying to explain that this was really not our intention; we were simply responding to a request from Vinesh who had been so helpful, so willing to support us and to make the hotel staff conscious of the importance of conserving the environment.

In need of a little tranquillity, we took our badly behaved selves to Labriz where Vinesh sat us down, ordered drinks and commiserated with us. He tried to find a compromise but in doing so ventured out onto the quick-sand with me, making life less comfortable for himself. He continued to send the gardeners to help us in the forest, opening a new area of overgrown cinnamon and coconut invaded hillside where it curved towards the bat roost. The coconuts were a particular problem; despite lying abandoned and unharvested for many years they were regarded as a protected species.

It was an easy task to clear the ground of fallen coconuts but the mature palms which would continue to drop nuts and fronds could not be felled without permission from the Forestry Department. Our intention was to remove about six coconut palms in this area and to replace them with endemic *Deckenia* palms. These elegant palms produce large dangling inflorescences of blossoms that attract many species of flying insects, a source of food for the sheath-tailed bats. By dealing with small patches of invaded forest we would, over the coming years, extend the rehabilitated forest closer to the bat roost.

We marked six coconut palms with bands of yellow plastic tape we had salvaged from the forgotten marker of the Grande Barbe road. A request was then made in writing to the director of the Ministry of Environment for the Forestry Division to come to Silhouette to verify that the palms we had marked could be felled. Their permission would enable us to show the owner which palms we were permitted to remove if he had no objection.

The edict of the feudal system under which the island was run was that all visitors, whether foreigners or Seychellois, required permission from the owner to visit the island. This included even members of the the government, like the man from the Forestry Division who, because we had requested his visit without prior approval, was refused permission although he was an official whose advice and approval was demanded by law.

If the coconuts were not removed, there was little point in trying to plant endemic palms and trees in their shadow because the falling fronds and nuts would destroy the new saplings.

It felt as though the quick-sand was slowly sucking me in deeper and deeper. The road, the National Park, the Labriz Science Committee and now a halt to our expansion of the lowland forest trail and improvements to the bat feeding territory. The best solution was to bury ourselves in our work. We still had to maintain the cleared and replanted areas in the forest and the groups of tourists needing guided walks did not diminish just because of our failings under the feudal system. Being busy also meant that no further mention was made of the earlier plan to transfer to Desroches island all the Aldabra tortoises. We desperately needed this to go ahead so that our two species of granite island giant tortoises would have Silhouette island to themselves. We waited patiently in anticipation of the right boat connection at the right time.

CHAPTER TWELVE

The avenue of bluish-green exotic palms that led from the road to the Dauban Mausoleum had, over the years, lost some of its elegance where several century old palms had abandoned their grip on the soil and fallen over. The seeds that had sprouted and taken root were not aligned as were the older trees, more clumped and haphazard, providing shelter and shade for the four Aldabra tortoises.

Earlier in the year some confusion about the shipping arrangements had led to the postponement of plans to transport these tortoises and their hatchlings to Desroches island. The four strong wooden crates for the adults had lain empty for months in anticipation of the voyage. In December, when Justin was on Silhouette, he organised, with the help of the island manager, to have the tortoises put into their crates. The hatchlings were removed from our juvenile enclosures and secured in large flat wooden boxes and taken down to the harbour to meet the supply boat on its brief stop en route for the outer islands and Desroches. With the Aldabra tortoises off the island, we were one step closer to our stated intention of releasing the granite island tortoises into the wild on Silhouette.

It was December 2009 and Justin was on his own, coping with the hotel guests who wanted to hike in the forest. He had the best part of two months' data to collect from the weather stations and data loggers. There were tortoises to weigh and measure, terrapin ponds to clean and reorganise following the release of six adult yellow-bellied terrapins into the hotel lake. There were bats to count and cameras to check. On top of these daily chores there was an annual general meeting of the Nature Protection Trust to organise. All this in our unexpectedly long absence from Silhouette.

In September, while we were on a short break in Cambridge, Gill had been diagnosed with cancer. At the end of that month, in the gap between the diagnosis and the start of treatment, we had returned to Silhouette, anxious to ensure the tortoises and terrapins would be cared for and to apologise to Vinesh for not being available for his hotel guests. We were unable to find volunteers at such short notice and our reliable regular volunteers Guy and Ann and Bill were not available for various reasons. Justin was supervising at Cambridge until late

November and none of the NPTS trustees were free to spend time on Silhouette.

Fortunately, Roc had a well-established routine and understood his responsibilities with regard to feeding the tortoises and cleaning the enclosures. The extra financial benefit we offered for the increased responsibility was, we hoped, an added incentive. The new island manager, Gilbert, was asked to keep an eye on the last batch of hatching eggs in the incubator and to put them in the relevant boxes where Roc would feed them. Several extra packets of Exoterra terrapin food that Guy had sent us were laid out in the laboratory for Roc to feed to the terrapins in the late afternoon – a five minute task.

The other projects we were responsible for, as set out in the annual work-plan we had been required to submit to the owner and ICS, could survive without intervention. The automatic weather stations and data loggers would continue to gather the data we needed for monitoring sooglossid frog habitats. The sheath-tailed bats would be left in peace and the cameras that spied on them would be turned off until an observer returned. The lowland forest trail was the only project needing constant attention that we would put on hold. The endemic plant seedlings for the project were not due to be planted out in the forest until the wet north-west monsoon weather at the end of the year when Justin was due to return.

It was our good fortune that during this difficult health crisis we were able to live in Gill's brother's flat in the small Northamptonshire town of Towcester. It was as far from the sea as one could possibly be in England, but the view from the flat was across a wide expanse of communal lawn to a tree-lined brook and beyond that, several acres of unkempt field. We threw bread out onto the path to attract the pheasants from the field, mallard from the brook, black-headed gulls so far from the sea, and gaggles of jackdaws. Very occasionally a small muntjac deer wandered hesitantly through the undergrowth along the brook.

Snow and the abbreviated days of winter came while Gill was recovering from surgery, prior to starting the debilitating course of chemotherapy. Those frosty silent days and later, when Gill lay in bed coping with the side effects of her treatment, gave me time to dream. It was a daydream of the warm Indian Ocean, the sound of the waves breaking over the outlying reef, the trade-wind rustling the palm fronds, but most all, a dream filled with the extraordinary landscape and wildlife on Silhouette. On those quiet days the daydreams were translated into rough watercolour drawings that slowly filled the pages of a large sketch pad.

There was a short reprieve between the end of the chemotherapy regime and a course of intravenous drugs that were to be given once every three weeks. We took advantage of this break to return to Silhouette and our commitments there in May 2009.

The house which had been unoccupied for the best part of four months was in need of a thorough spring clean. The tortoises and terrapins looked healthy and had obviously been fed and cleaned. The air conditioned Information Centre was as we had left it and was, for the next two weeks, open for business.

At the hotel we caught up with the developments these past months and Vinesh gave us the news that his dedicated hawksbill turtle monitoring staff had reported a good nesting season. We were able to tell him that Gill's new medication would allow us to spend more time on Silhouette over the next few months and that we anticipated a permanent return by December at the latest.

We were to make three more short trips in that time and Justin two more trips on his own, so that after May between us we were present for at least two weeks every month. It was fortunate that we had insurance to pay for Gill's treatment but the travel expenses were considerable.

When, in August, we arrived for a two-week stay, it was to find that four days before our return the island had been officially declared a National Park. There was a small stone plinth where the President had made the declaration. Across the road a large new signboard extolled the values of the Silhouette National Park and acknowledged the dedicated work of the Ministry of Environment, National Parks Board, IDC and Labriz hotel. With the exception of the input of the hotel, their specific contributions towards the founding of the park appeared to be little more than the erection of the sign.

There was, however, no time to ponder our apparent invisibility because early in the morning after our return to Silhouette the island manager came to alert us to a minor tragedy. On the day of the national park declaration, two or three children had managed to break some strands of the steel mesh cover over one of our hatchling tortoise enclosures. Using a metal spike, they had speared several very small baby tortoises. Four were missing, two dead in the enclosure and two slightly injured. We were apparently responsible for the incident because, had we been on Silhouette, the children would not have ventured into the enclosure. These children, juvenile thugs, whoever they were, disappeared into the protective arms of their parents and there were no repercussions. A careful examination of the hatchlings in the enclosure; inspecting their shells, their skinny little legs and delicate claws, revealed that other than the two with minor injuries, all the other inhabitants had survived unscathed.

Vinesh came to see us a few days before we were due to leave again. He was not his usual cheerful self but, in any case, was happy to tell us that some of the marked terrapins had been seen in the hotel lake. The real news, though, was that Labriz was to have a new temporary manager from the Hilton hotels group and that he and Bernali were leaving Seychelles. It was news we really did not want hear. We would miss the good neighbourly relationship we had built with them and the hotel. Would we be able to have an equally friendly arrangement with a globalised company like Hilton? Time would tell.

Our relationship with Hilton was the subject of serious discussion when we returned for a short spell in September. We and the hotel management were asked to attend a meeting organised by a government delegation on a mission to fulfil one of their commitments under the UNDP/GEF project, seeking to encourage tourism operators to work with conservation organisations.

The general manager and his head of maintenance were keen to assure us and the delegation that they were more than willing to continue to support our conservation projects. This seemed to bode well for our future relationship with the new hotel management.

There was another cooperative venture underway on the Dauban marsh. The solitary grey heron had become all flustered and flushed when a healthy female heron took up residence on his otherwise fiercely defended marsh territory. He blushed bright red across his bill and down his legs all the way to his feet. He began collecting sticks to build her a nest in a clump of mangrove ferns. She laid two eggs for him and they set about raising the first grey heron chicks we had ever seen on Silhouette.

In the final weeks of Gill's

treatment in England and before the tests that would give us the all-clear to return to Silhouette, I put the finishing touches to the watercolour illustrations and text for the book I had dreamt about in those cold, quiet days of last winter. The book would be filled with reminders of the fascinating natural history along the most visited trail through the forest to Jardin Marrons.

It would feature a little human history, the natural history of the shoreline, landscapes and and open landscapes but also the remarkable cluster of weather-beaten rocks on the trail that resembled gigantic fossil remains, from a Jurassic age, the palms, orchids, pitcher plants and the exquisitely beautiful ephemeral hypoxidia flowers, fruit bats, geckos, chameleons, butterflies and the trees that dominated this amazing tropical forest. The book would, I hoped, help us raise funds by appealing to the many visitors who accompanied me on guided walks. With generous support from Peter Kistler's SAN organisation, the book, "An Island Lost in Time", was printed and ready for our permanent return to Silhouette.

When Gill was given the "all clear" in November, we packed our bags and left the flat in Towcester. At Gatwick airport we unburdened ourselves of fourteen months of car hire and boarded a flight away from a very dark and gloomy November day. There seemed to be a big rush to get us all seated and the aircraft away to the starting line. The moment we became airborne, we disappeared into the complete white-out of a blizzard that held us in its embrace until we emerged into a clear blue sky.

"This is your captain speaking", came over the cabin loudspeakers. "You may be interested to know that Gatwick and Heathrow have both been closed to all flights because of the snow-storm. We were the last aircraft to leave."

This was a good omen for us on our way home at last.

There was a disturbed rolling north-westerly wind-driven sea on the passage between Mahé and Silhouette that added to the fatigue of the long journey. Disembarking at six-thirty in the evening, our one and only thought was to have a light snack and to creep into bed.

There were no dramas to greet us the next beautiful sunny morning, a world away from the cold snowy winter we had left behind. Roc was all smiles now that the responsibility for the tortoises had been lifted from his shoulders. We made a leisurely tour of inspection of the tortoise enclosures where the tortoises all appeared to be in perfect condition. The terrapins came up to the surface of their ponds, expecting to be fed. The herons were fishing along the edge of the marsh, their two well-grown chicks waiting patiently for breakfast. When we finished sorting things out in the Information Centre, we found a young French couple, Cedric and Katarina, the new managers of "La Belle Tortue" waiting to introduce themselves.

Later in the day we took ourselves off to see Daniella at the Eco Center and then to Labriz to see Tom, the temporary general manager. We reported our permanent return and offered my services as guide for visitors wanting to visit Jardin Marron. He was particularly happy to know that the tortoises and the Information Centre would be fully manned for the visit two days hence of the cruise ship "Columbus". Apparently the hotel was now handling the cruise ships and were also likely to be benefitting from the landing fees. In the past, the cruise ships had been small expedition cruises with around one hundred passengers. We had handled their shore excursions, releasing the island manager of any responsibility other than collecting the landing fees from the shipping agent. Over the years we have escorted over 5,000 cruise ship passengers on shore excursions, earning the island and its owner a sizeable income.

On that first full day back on Silhouette we were pleased to be approached by hotel guests wanting to report that they had watched a turtle nesting at Anse Patates. In the afternoon another couple came by with a very exhausted bee-eater which they have found at Anse Lascars. We could hear the bee-eaters calling somewhere high up over the forest, but they did not appear to be part of an invasion as large as that of a few years earlier.

At dusk we did the usual evening rounds, checking the tortoises and terrapins and taking a quick look at the bats on the CCTV cameras. They were in four groups, difficult to count with any accuracy but probably numbering 25 to 30 bats.

The chores over, we had a quiet supper and retired to bed, tired but happy to be home. Next morning I was busy in the kitchen with breakfast when the island manager came up the two steps onto the verandah and knocked on the screen door.

"I've got a letter from the office for you", he said, waving the envelope in my direction.

The letter, dated 1st December, was addressed to me with copies to the island manager, ICS, Silhouette Foundation and the Hilton Labriz manager. It said, in essence, that the owner had decided to appoint Silhouette Foundation as conservation manager on Silhouette.

"Therefore, it is with some regret that IDC has decided it is in the best interest of Silhouette conservation to give NPTS notice and request that you vacate the IDC premises you currently occupy.......We will allow you to retain the facilities until the end of the year". The end of the year was exactly twenty-seven days away. We were being given less than one month's notice of eviction after fourteen years of voluntary unpaid service to conservation on Silhouette.

    The letter then reminded us that we had been provided with free accommodation, a building to house the laboratory, the Information Centre and shop. (No mention that it had been a dilapidated ruin that we had renovated with funds from an overseas donor) and that we had provided with "significant manpower to assist with day to day conservation". (We had only ever had Jules and then Roc for about two hours each day to help with the tortoises. There had never been "manpower" to help with other projects.)

    The closing paragraph included a magnanimous gesture allowing us to continue working on Silhouette under the direction of Silhouette Foundation, (overlooking the demand that we vacate not only the house but the Information Centre where we worked). A final patronising sentence suggested I was now of retiring age and wished me a happy retirement.

    Although the warning signs had been there for some time, this imperious, cruel letter, completely lacking in compassion for the difficult situation we had been through during the year, read like a death sentence. It threatened to put an end to everything we had worked for and believed in for the last two decades of dedication to conservation.

    It wasn't in our nature to simply roll over and accept being evicted from Silhouette. I tried to arrange a meeting to discuss the letter but was only granted an appointment with one of the board members four days later. Gill and I wrote an immediate reply to the letter. We said that we were more than willing to pay rent for the house and the Information Centre. We reminded him that over the years we had earned our keep by handling all shore excursions for the cruise ships and day visitors. We reiterated that we fully understood and accepted that we were now subservient to Silhouette Foundation for all new projects. And finally, a brief reminder that our periods of absence this year were as a result of Gill's cancer treatment which no-one could have foreseen.

    In an attempt to fight for our conservation projects, we thought of every possible organisation and individual who had ever worked with us. Letters were sent and phone calls made to anyone in government we thought might have influence with the owner. There were absolutely no positive responses from government and not one of our colleagues in the local conservation community spoke up for us. We thought this was probably due to their dependence on government support and their members often being government staff. Appeals to reverse the eviction order were made to the Minister for the Environment by many of our international scientific colleagues and supporters, but also to no avail. In reply to these appeals the Ministry produced a standardised letter in which we were accused of being uncooperative with "the new institutional framework and programme", whatever that meant!

The Minister also claimed that I was partly responsible for preventing other NGOs from working on Silhouette. With the exception of one minor incident in fourteen years, we had worked closely with all scientists, conservation groups and school field trips that had been permitted to visit Silhouette.

In January 2010, at a final meeting with the owner and the head of the conservation department, it was apparent that there was no way back, the decision to evict us and all the tortoises was set in stone. The only concession, as a result of our lobbying, was an extension to our departure date. The new date was two and a half months away, at the end of March.

In order to appear conciliatory, they suggested that we could keep our conservation projects running once we had relocated to somewhere on Mahé. This really made no sense at all, especially so under the threat that the Information Centre would be demolished in May. Even if we had the use of the Centre we were a purely voluntary NGO and did not have the corporate structure of the other NGOs with paid staff we could send to the island. It was we who did the physical work and wasting time commuting was definitely not feasible. The prospect of abandoning our conservation projects was overshadowed by the urgent need to deal with the giant tortoise problem. From the very beginning, we had clearly stated that the captive breeding project was intended to repopulate Silhouette with its natural herbivore species. Neither government nor the owner had every objected. Until now. The reason put forward for excluding the tortoises from the environment was that they would be stolen, completely overlooking the fact that, since 2006, five healthy *Arnoldi* tortoises were living in the wild at Grande Barbe and that there were numerous wild tortoises on North, Fregate, Cousin and Cousine islands. A last minute appeal to reconsider this diktat was made at an ICS meeting by Gerard Rocamora, a colleague whose terrapins we had looked after prior to their release on North island. His intervention on our behalf failed because of the dominating influence the owner held in that organisation and the total lack of support from the other ICS members we had considered to be our friends.

Thus ended the patronising, often petulant, letters and phone calls that treated us like misbehaving children. It was time to stop fighting and to start packing

The most important subject, needing immediate attention, was to find somewhere to send 180 tortoises. Having come this far on the assumption that we had bred the two original species from the granite islands, we did not want to send them all to one island where they would once again become an amorphous herd of giant tortoises. The unfortunate truth, though, was that wherever they went they would once more be mixed with Aldabra tortoises. We decided that in the event of future research into their species relationship with the Aldabra tortoises all our juvenile tortoises should be fitted with microchips for easy identification. The microchips, which were kindly donated by a member of the British Chelonia Group, were inserted under the loose skin of the upper part of the hind legs.

The conservation team on North island, our nearest neighbouring island, responded immediately when asked if they would accept all the *Arnoldi* juvenile tortoises. As an acknowledgement of their prompt response we included, with the tortoises, our entire specimen collection and the cabinets in which it was housed.

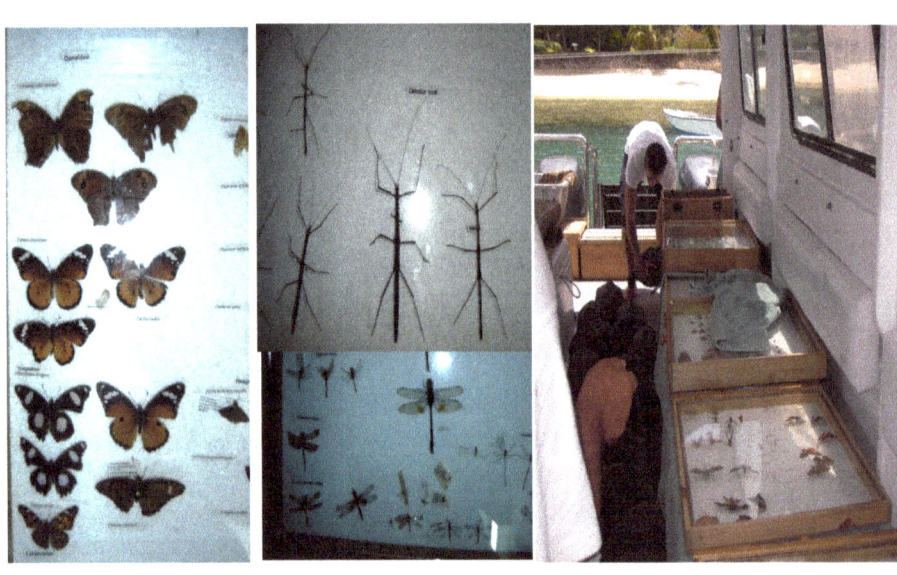

Our second, but equally important, choice of islands where we knew they had tortoises was Cousine island. Like North, Cousine is a reasonably-sized island with one small very exclusive hotel. Their own tortoises, including two large old *Hololissa* males, lived in the wild. Much to our relief they were equally enthusiastic about receiving all the adult and juvenile *Hololissa* tortoises.

Halfway through the transfer of tortoises to North island, the new Russian owner of the North's hotel decided that there were already too many tortoises on the island and refused his conservation staff permission to accept any more. The alternative was for us to approach Fregate island, another privately owned hotel island, with a well established herd of free-ranging Aldabra tortoises. They were more than willing to accept our offer of 94 juvenile *Arnoldis* but with the proviso that they would only be able to collect them in May, which posed a problem for us because we would no longer be based on Silhouette. On the understanding that the tortoises would all be removed from the island, permission was grudgingly given for them to remain in the enclosures until the end of May. Roc would continue to feed them and we would have to commute from Mahé to look after them three or four days a week.

The terrapin project was comparatively easy to close down as we had only nine yellow-bellied terrapins in the enclosures. Justin took them to the freshwater lake at the hotel where he had previously released terrapins. The release was conducted in the presence of a small crowd of hotel guests and staff to whom Justin gave an explanatory talk. We offered to give the terrapin enclosures to the school, thinking it could serve as a small plant nursery for their nature classes, but unfortunately they were not interested.

Justin had retrieved all the automatic weather stations and data loggers from the forest and together we had unravelled the CCTV cameras and cables from the bat roost. North island came to collect the drawers of fragile specimens and the bulky cabinet.

It took us two months to pack our belongings and all the office and laboratory equipment into whatever dilapidated cardboard boxes we could find. The hotel obligingly bought our antique furniture to put in the Grande Case, we sold the washing machine and refrigerator and gave Roc our comfy old Laura Ashley sofa. With the laboratory stripped of its equipment we set up a temporary kitchen for the days when we would be commuting to the island.

At the eleventh hour, on the last day of March, Cousine island's conservation manager arrived in a boat to collect the *Hololissa* tortoises.

It was heartbreaking to see them gone, almost like sending our family or our favourite pets to somewhere we knew we would never ever see them again. The remaining tortoises destined for Fregate were all juveniles in the smaller secure enclosures, leaving the main enclosure empty and forlorn.

The first week in April, having vacated the house, we spent in the luxury of the Hilton Labriz hotel while the shipping of our belongings to Mahé was organised. We had found a furnished house to rent at Anse aux Pins and bought a second-hand car, our first car in twenty years. Once our goods and chattels were delivered and had been arranged in our new abode, we began the long commute to Silhouette every two or three days. It soon became obvious that we could not have continued our conservation projects under these circumstances. The commute involved a three quarter hour drive to Bel Ombre, an unspecified wait for the boat to leave and half an hour making the crossing through the early stages of the trade-wind driven sea. We arrived at the Information Centre a little worse for wear at somewhere between eleven and midday, in need of a cup of coffee. After lunch we tidied up, checked the remaining tortoises and were ready for the return journey around four in the afternoon. We staggered on, trying to make the best of these unsatisfactory visits all through April and May and into early June when we were informed by the hotel manager that he was under instruction to deny us access to Silhouette on the hotel ferry service.

In the months before being banished from Silhouette, it became glaringly apparent that the empty enclosures bereft of their giant tortoises were not an attraction for the hotel guests. With the decline in visitors went the drop in sales of the fund-raising items for NPTS and our own life support, our craftwork. The new book of water-colours "An Island Lost in Time", upon which we had placed so much hope for the future, sat in an unwanted pile as did the Silhouette Guide we had published some years earlier.

There were days when our sympathetic neighbours, Cedric and Katarina invited us over to "La Belle Tortue" for lunch to give us a break from our project demolition work. Katarina had also offered to open the door of the Information Centre for visitors on the days when we were not present on the island.

When, at the beginning of June, the boat from Fregate came to collect the remaining tortoises, we had no reason to continue the commute to Silhouette. Our last visit was a short "thank-you" favour for Cedric and Katarina who were in need of a few days holiday in Mauritius. "La Belle Tortue" was without guests, so that we had a luxurious room at our disposal and the use of an entire professional kitchen and the empty restaurant to rattle about in.

The last trace of our presence in the Information Centre was packed into a bag ready to take back to Mahé. That done, we realised that for the first time in fourteen years we had no conservation chores to attend to. On this, our last day on Silhouette, we had time to wander up the road past the Dauban mausoleum, pausing briefly under the perfumed clusters of flowers on the ylang-ylang tree, and on to the glacis above Anse Lascars. We saw one of the kestrels on the crumbling cliff above the glacis, listened to the clacking call of the tropic-birds and watched a lonely frigate bird wheeling above the bay on its scimitar wings. In humus-filled depressions in the solid granite slope of the glacis, tangles of pandanus, canthium and grass flourished and, as if struggling to reach these pockets of life, long strands of beach morning glory crept up the wrinkles in the rock-face.

The sea was the purest pure blue, its waves, piling up ahead of the strengthening trade-winds, were breaking on the outlying coral reef, sending wispy clouds of spray drifting up into the forest-covered mountains. We, two solitary figures, sought solace in this uninhabited landscape that appeared as unsullied and innocent as it had been when first seen by those two small sailing ships of the East India Company in 1609.

POSTSCRIPT

In much the same way as those East Indiamen came to the islands, refreshed themselves and then continued on their journey, leaving behind only a written journal or two as witness to their visit, so it was with us. With the exception of the Silhouette National Park, whatever we achieved on Silhouette has since been obliterated as though we had never set foot on the island. And again, like John Jourdain's 1609 journal, that is what will remain of our fourteen years of voluntary conservation work; written records and several publications.

Justin's contribution to the wider interest in the biodiversity of all the Seychelles islands is, however, much more significant. The species monographs he wrote and edited in collaboration with many specialist taxonomists will provide future researchers with the necessary data on the distribution of all known species.

As for Gill and myself, we thoroughly enjoyed the years we lived on Silhouette, the pleasure of introducing so many people to aspects of the natural history of the island and giving them the opportunity to discover that giant tortoises are charismatic, friendly animals that enjoy a human touch.

Our "Stan"
living wild on Silhouette since 2006

www.ingramcontent.com/pod-product-compliance
Lightning Source LLC
Chambersburg PA
CBHW040336300426
44113CB00021B/2761